Nation to Nation

Aboriginal Sovereignty and the Future of Canada

**DIANE ENGELSTAD
AND JOHN BIRD**

Editors

First published in 1992 by
House of Anansi Press Limited
1800 Steeles Avenue West
Concord, Ontario
L4K 2P3

Canadian Cataloguing in Publication Data

Main entry under title:

Nation to nation : aboriginal sovereignty & the future of Canada

ISBN 0-88784-533-9

1. Native peoples — Canada — Government relations —
1951-   .*   I. Engelstad, Diane.   II. Bird, John, 1953-   .

E92.N38 1992   323.1'197071   C92-095368-9

Cover design: Brant Cowie/ArtPlus Limited
Typesetting: Tony Gordon Ltd.

Printed and bound in Canada

House of Anansi Press gratefully acknowledges the support of the
Canada Council, Ontario Ministry of Culture and Communications,
Ontario Arts Council, and Ontario Publishing Centre in the
development of writing and publishing in Canada.

For John Olthuis,
an inspiration to many
to stand in solidarity with
aboriginal people

CONTENTS

II Communities in Transition

ACKNOWLEDGEMENTS

W<small>E WOULD LIKE TO THANK</small> the members of the editorial committee and the staff of Citizens for Public Justice, who were always ready to assist and offer support; we are particularly indebted to Andrew Brouwer, who devoted countless hours of assistance and served as our "sounding board" as we pulled together the final manuscript.

We gratefully acknowledge financial support for development of the book from Church of the Holy Trinity (Toronto), In Response (Toronto) and the supporters of Citizens for Public Justice.

We would also like to thank:

the contributors, who graciously gave us their trust and co-operation,

Kathryn Dean, for her invaluable editorial assistance, and our manuscript readers for their helpful critiques,

Virginia Smith, for her original vision and the book's early development,

our families, for their patience, support and good ideas,

all aboriginal people who have journeyed with us, shared their humanity with us and thus helped bring us to the point of creating this book.

PREFACE

I MUST HAVE BEEN one of the first in line at the government bookstore in Toronto when Justice Thomas Berger's *Report of the Mackenzie Valley Pipeline Inquiry* came out in 1977. I was a university student, angry about a lot of things, but especially, at that time, about the government's ongoing shabby treatment of native people. Like many other Canadians, I knew we couldn't wash our hands of destroying the cultural fabric and livelihood of the Mackenzie Valley just to meet the south's voracious appetite for non-renewable resources. The *Berger Report* did not disappoint. In its pages I met the people of the North whose eloquent statements about their relationship to the land and to one another affected me deeply and filled me with respect.

I followed the saga of the Berger Inquiry, National Energy Board assessment hearings and government flip-flops on whether we were, or were not, running out of gas supplies, with help from an organization called the Committee for Justice and Liberty — the organization that initiated the book you are about to read. This relatively small national citizens' group, now known as Citizens for Public Justice (CPJ), drew most of its support at the time from Dutch protestants who had immigrated to Canada in the 1950s. The fact that it was small and from a minority community didn't discourage the group in the least from tackling big issues in a big way. In the tradition, perhaps, of holding back the sea with a few well-constructed dikes, CPJ went head to head with the National Energy Board in 1975 and had Marshall Crowe ousted from the chair for potential conflict of interest due to his connections with Canadian Arctic Gas. For CPJ, it was simply a question of justice, and the core group worked hard to communicate to its members what was at stake for all Canadians if we were to tolerate injustice.

I'm not really sure whether my connection with CPJ — I was raised in the Dutch Calvinist tradition — galvanized my interest in aboriginal issues, or whether my interest in aboriginal issues led to a long-term association with CPJ. In any case, I came to identify the organization's approach to public issues as my own. Central to the approach was the idea that the biblical injunction to "love thy neighbour" had a key role to play in politics, economics and all the other systems human beings instituted. That principle seemed to offer a fresh — we liked to use the word "radical" — perspective on how to create a more inclusive and caring society.

What I gained from CPJ's approach to the pipeline issue, more than anything else, I think, was the recognition that it was not my place as a well-meaning Christian to define what "justice" would mean for the Dene of the Northwest Territories or other people. "Justice" meant uncluttering our social structures and institutions of the cultural baggage that prevented people like the Dene from having control over their lives and their communities. All people have a right, and a responsibility, CPJ said, to live according to their convictions and values. Justice for one community ultimately means justice for the Canadian social fabric as a whole.

Another key tenet of CPJ's approach to public issues was the biblical concept of "stewardship": the notion that we are caretakers, not owners, of the earth and its resources. It was on this basis that CPJ critiqued the wastefulness of Canada's energy policy and challenged the assumption of many Canadians that our "standard of living" required ever new non-renewable sources of energy. Working with aboriginal groups, CPJ met people who understood far more about living in harmony with the earth than theories of "stewardship" could ever express.

Involvement with the Dene in the Mackenzie Valley Pipeline issue led CPJ to subsequent involvement in aboriginal struggles elsewhere in Canada. CPJ assisted efforts towards a settlement of mercury pollution claims of the Anishnabai, or Ojibway, of Grassy Narrows in northwestern Ontario. Further connections were made with the Teme-Augama Anishnabai at Bear Island in Lake Temagami (northeastern Ontario) in that people's fight for recognition of their traditional lands and with the Innu Nation in Labrador in opposing low-level military flights over traditional, unceded territory. These connections and involvements have been worked out largely through the commitment and personality of John Olthuis, a founding member of CPJ and its Research Director for many years. John Olthuis is now a lawyer whose practice is devoted to supporting aboriginal peoples in their political struggles for self-determination. Other CPJ staff and members have also been involved in support of First Nations, particularly with the Lubicon Cree in northern Alberta and the Ingenika in the northern interior of British Columbia.

This book comes out of CPJ's participation in such efforts, and reflects the liaisons that have formed between people — both native and non-native — committed to aboriginal justice.

Both John Bird and I, the editors, are former national staff members of CPJ. Our own involvement with aboriginal issues has grown through our vocational experiences, pre-CPJ, with CPJ and post-CPJ. We come to the task of putting together this book through personal interest, and through a conviction, shared with CPJ, that is both spiritual and political. We believe we hear the whispered voice of the Spirit in the cries of both native and non-native people for justice and new relationships. We also believe that in responding together to the Spirit, we may find ourselves leaving our prisons of pain and guilt to dance in the circle of life, face to face, nation to nation.

DIANE ENGELSTAD

INTRODUCTION

ELIJAH HARPER AND OKA changed everything for us. The relationship between the First Nations[1] and the rest of the people in what we now call Canada is no longer as it was before the summer of 1990.

We cannot ignore what Elijah Harper did. He broadsided the Meech Lake Accord, one of the most significant constitutional processes in modern Canadian history, for the simple and unequivocal reason that it did not address the marginalization of the First Nations in the structural relations of the country.

We cannot ignore Oka. The events that took place there in 1990 revealed the undercurrent of greed and racism in Canadian society. The absurdity of several thousand troops with tanks and helicopters laying siege to tiny Kanesatake to "defend" the town of Oka's "right" to build a golf course on the sacred heartland of the few remaining Mohawk acres would be laughable were it not so horrifying.

So now, nothing is as it was before. Some governments are beginning to accept the validity of aboriginal political power. And in the constitutional talks of 1992, aboriginal leaders have won for themselves a more significant and respected place at the table than ever before, from which they have been able to advocate their inherent right to self-government. Broad public pressure for a just settlement of native grievances has encouraged politicians to take the matter seriously. Most non-native Canadians have begun to see that they can no longer pretend the situation of the First Nations is a minor problem our governments can continue to sidestep with more money or promises while they focus on "more important" problems.

Nor can the rest of Canada pretend that the problems facing aboriginal peoples are the result of laziness or of some innate inferiority. Such easily held, racist assumptions are, thankfully, harder to find these days than in the past.

Canadians are starting to acknowledge that the cheating, robbery and shunting aside of indigenous peoples by Europeans and their descendants is at the heart of the malaise that threatens to break the country apart. Until we address together the foundational injustices upon which our shared colonial history and present situation are based, we won't be the kind of nation we like to think we are. We may well, in fact, find it difficult to be a nation at all.

Thanks to Elijah and Oka and many others both before and after that pivotal summer of 1990, there is a new spirit of pride and dignity among the aboriginal peoples. And there is a renewed vision and determination to continue the push for justice.

The media are paying more attention now. The politicians are paying more attention. We are all paying more attention. More and more of the terrible stories are being told — from the points of view of those who have been wronged. That is good, for there is much to learn, not only about what was lost, but also about new hopes and aspirations rooted in the traditional teachings of the elders.

This book contains some of those stories. In addition, you will find reflections, by both native and non-native authors, on how we arrived at our present predicament and how we might find solutions together. The storytelling and analysis are intertwined, since both are needed to move us beyond rhetoric to a new relationship.

In Part I, native and non-native authors describe what has happened along the road to sovereignty so far, and what key changes are required. As the authors point out, self-government has spiritual, economic, cultural and political dimensions, and they need to be dealt with holistically.

Part II provides examples of how aboriginal people have been working out their visions of sovereignty and self-determination within the realities of their own communities.

Because this book is especially about changing the non-aboriginal structures that stand in the way of sovereignty, Part

III looks at the role of non-native support for aboriginal rights. Gary Potts, Chief of the Teme-Augama Anishnabai Nation, offers his perspective in light of the Temagami struggle, which involved the aboriginal community, environmentalist groups and the forestry industry. In other articles, non-native Canadians who have committed great amounts of time and energy to "solidarity" work over the years reflect on their experience and what they have learned.

Nothing is as it was before. That can be threatening. But it is also what we find exciting and hopeful about this period of history.

JOHN BIRD

I

THE ROAD BACK TO SOVEREIGNTY: VOICES FROM TWO CULTURES

GEORGES ERASMUS AND
JOE SANDERS

CANADIAN HISTORY: AN ABORIGINAL PERSPECTIVE

ABORIGINAL SOVEREIGNTY

WHEN NON-NATIVE PEOPLE first came to this continent some five hundred years ago, indigenous peoples lived all across the Americas. It is a matter of historical record that before the arrival of Europeans, these First Nations possessed and exercised absolute sovereignty over what is now called the North American continent. Hundreds of tribal communities, made up of a variety of nations and representing at least ten linguistic groups, lived in what is now known as Canada, from Newfoundland to Vancouver Island.

It was not possible to find "empty" land in the Americas. All the land was being used by the First Nations. Our people decided their own citizenship. They had a wide variety and diversity of governmental systems, almost all of them regulating their activities and the relations among their members with a degree of formality. The way they dealt with the Europeans is ample proof of their capacity to enter into relations with foreign powers: they made a number of treaties with the French and British Crowns, and many of the colonies survived because of the assistance First Nations gave to the European settlers.

Our people knew how to survive in this part of the world. They knew all of their valleys and mountains and rivers. They had names in their own languages for all of these places. They believed that all things had their place, from even the smallest insect and the smallest leaf. And they were taught to respect life and all living things. Our people were living lives that must have been of a much higher quality than people now live in Canada.

It was unfortunate that early Christian leaders believed that our people did not understand why human beings were here on earth. Our people did not think there were gods in every leaf. But they did think that everything around was given by the Creator. They believed that there was one supreme being, that there was purpose in all of this, and that the purpose did not end when we died.

Our people were not a war-like people, but they did defend their interests. Our territorial boundaries were clearly defined. Although First Nations had many disputes with neighbours in their history, they eventually arrived at peaceful arrangements with one another.

Our people understood what the non-native people were after when they came amongst our people and wanted to treaty with them, because they had done that many times amongst themselves. They recognized that a nation-to-nation agreement, defining the specific terms of peaceful coexistence, was being arranged.

BROKEN AGREEMENTS

When our people treatied with another nation, each nation's interests, its pride, and its word were at stake. The word of the agreement, the treaty, was given in a very sacred way. And it was not very easily broken.

So it was quite amazing to our people — and it took them a long, long time to realize — that they could sit with other people whose religious leaders were present, and who would be virtually lying to our people as they were executing the treaty. Even before the document reached London or Paris or Ottawa, they were already forgetting the solemn promises they had made. That never happened on the side of the indigenous people.

It didn't help that the European interpretation of a treaty, often differing radically from the First Nation's interpretation or understanding, significantly altered the intent of the original agreement. For example, ownership of land in the Anglo-Canadian "fee simple" sense of title was foreign to the thinking and systems of First Nations. Land was revered as a mother from which life came, and was to be preserved for future generations as it had been from time immemorial. Land was used for common benefit, with no individual having a right to any more of it than another. A nation's traditional hunting grounds were recognized by its neighbours as "belonging" to that nation, but this was different from the idea of private ownership. For the most part, the boundaries were not delineated, although some nations in British Columbia had systems of identifying their boundaries and passing on custodial responsibilities. First Nations peoples, then and now, believe that they live *with* the land, not simply on it.

As our people understood it, they had agreed to allow peaceful settlement by non-native people in large parts of their valleys and mountains and on rivers, but at the same time native people would retain large tracts of land on which they would govern themselves; on which our institutions would continue to survive; where we would nurture our children; where our languages and our culture would flourish; where we could continue our lives; where we could hunt if we wished, plant crops if we wished, fish if we wished. And where, if we wanted to, we could also be educated in a formal way to become doctors, lawyers or whatever we wished.

The history of the settlement of Canada shows that non-native people, represented by federal, provincial and local governments, have continued to break the original agreements. Hunting, fishing, trapping and gathering sections of treaties that were to protect the aboriginal way of life have continued to be changed by Canadian government policies, regulations and legislation. The original land base agreed to at treaty time has continued to be expropriated for bridges, municipal expansion, military exercises and railway and highway right-of-ways, generally without compensation. In many cases, First Nations are still waiting to have the land entitlement of one-hundred-year-old treaties fulfilled.

REWRITING HISTORY

Non-native people have even distorted history. It is very difficult to find a history textbook in any province of this country that accurately tells the story of how our two peoples came together. Instead, there are books in which we are still being called pagans and savages, without an accurate reflection of the solemn agreements that were made and which indicate that indigenous people were to continue to govern themselves.

Native people have the enormous job of tapping people on the shoulder and saying, "This is not the way it's supposed to be. This is not the way we are supposed to be coexisting. We aren't supposed to be the poorest of the poor in our land." Our people have an understanding of the early agreements that the school books usually ignore.

In 1763, three years after the French and British resolved their differences in Canada and recognized Britain as the European power here, the Crown of Great Britain laid down a process in the Royal Proclamation that set forth the Crown's policy on land negotiations. That policy has never been revoked. In the Royal Proclamation, the Crown recognized that any lands possessed by First Nations in what was then British North America, would be reserved for them, unless, or until, they ceded that land to the Crown.

The Proclamation could be regarded as the first major legal link between First Nations and the British Crown. And by virtue of that Proclamation, it can be said that First Nations became protected states of the British, while being recognized as sovereign nations competent to maintain the relations of peace and war and capable of governing themselves under that protection.

Under international law, a weaker power does not surrender its right to self-government merely by associating with a stronger power and taking its protection.

Between 1781 and Canadian Confederation in 1867, some First Nations signed treaties with the Crown under which they ceded rights and privileges to certain lands. In return, they were to obtain certain treaty rights. These treaties represented further legal links between those nations and the Crown. But again, there is no evidence that sovereignty was surrendered.

Canadian courts, since the latter part of the nineteenth century, have relegated the First Nations' treaties with the Crown almost to the level of private law contracts, thereby denying their status as treaties in the sense of international law. Yet the Supreme Court of Canada repeated in the *R. v. Simon* case that First Nations' treaties are unique and share some of the features of international treaties. If the agreements were "treaties among sovereign nations" in the eighteenth and nineteenth centuries, how could their status be changed without the consent of First Nations?

In 1867, the British North America Act (later renamed the Constitution Act 1867) provided for internal self-government in Canada by European settlers. First Nations were not a party to the Confederation that was established, nor to the drafting of the British North America Act. Nevertheless, subsection 91(24) provided that the federal Parliament would have the authority to legislate for "Indians and lands reserved for the Indians" to the exclusion of the provincial legislatures. By virtue of that subsection, the First Nations were placed under the legislative power of the federal government as agent of the Crown, but not under its territorial jurisdiction.

Certain other treaties were executed between some of the First Nations and the Crown after Confederation. In many cases it is evident that treaties were imposed upon First Nations and that their leaders had little choice but to consent. The treaties were written in English and the Crown's negotiators often misrepresented the contents.

Today it may be argued that many of those treaties are "unequal" or "unconscionable" or "unfair" in both substance and procedure. Even so, First Nations did not perceive the treaties as being a surrender of sovereignty.

THE INDIAN ACT

In 1876, the federal government passed its first Indian Act, "the first consolidation of the laws pertaining to Indians." The Indian Act was passed by the federal government because it had exclusive legislative responsibility for Indians and lands reserved for Indians, but First Nations themselves had no input into it. Neither did First Nations' citizens have any part in electing the politicians who legislated the Indian Acts, since native people were not allowed to vote federally until 1960.

In the early days of European settlement, it is likely that native self-government continued for some time because First Nations had the numbers and the strength at that time to warrant recognition. But as time went on, that changed. During the first sixty years of this century, our people were in the most despicable, colonizing, racist situation imaginable. Under the control of Indian agents, they could not leave their reserves without passes. They were not legally in charge of a single thing that happened on their land.

The same Department of Indian Affairs that controlled our lives through Indian agents until only recently still exists today. It has 4000 civil servants, and its primary function is to maintain control over native people.

The Indian Act still controls every facet of our lives. It allows a certain amount of local self-government, but there is not a single thing on which we can make a law that does not have to go to a department official. That official is usually a bureaucrat whose face we've never seen and who has never seen the community. And yet he has total power to determine whether he is going to pass a dog law, a local development law, a garbage law or any law requiring departmental approval. He doesn't have to give a reason; he can just deny it. No other municipal government in this country is up against that kind of control. Surely it only exists in parts of the world where an occupying army wants to ensure that the population is completely submissive.

Today, every time we see a movement beginning among indigenous people somewhere in this country, the Department of Indian Affairs finds some way to divide those people — discredit their organization, discredit their leadership, create an opposition group, fund an opposition group.

Some day the Department of Indian Affairs should vanish off the face of the earth. There must be a time when the kind of colonial, dictatorial control that is ruining our lives comes to an end. We must have freedom at some point.

RETAINING OUR RIGHTS: THE ONGOING SAGA

Despite all of this, the Royal Proclamation of 1763 is still alive and well. That means that where there are no treaties the land belongs to the First Nations, and no Canadian government — whether provincial or federal — should be developing our resources and extracting royalties and taxes from them. There should be indigenous governments and institutions for aboriginal people.

In some cases in this country, we have treaties over a hundred years old by which, very clearly, original land was to have been set aside for native people. After a hundred years and more, the land still hasn't been put aside. Meanwhile, governments have repeatedly invited people from all over the world to come cut down our trees and get a square mile . . . two square miles . . . ten square miles of land. Although everyone agrees that our people have lived here for thousands of years, because the federal government has not recognized First Nations' title, there is not a square centimetre that is recognized as indigenous territory.

First Nations regularly confront governments with their claims to entitlement, and the governments can't deny the validity of such claims. But instead of recognizing land as indigenous territory, they seek to "settle" claims by exchanging historic rights for "fee simple" ownership, so the land can be treated like every other piece of private property in Canada.

Take, for example, the territory we call Denendeh, otherwise known as the western Northwest Territories. The Dene know they have always owned this land, but the federal government refuses to acknowledge our indigenous title. Recently the smallest group of Dene, the Gwitch'in, negotiated an agreement with the federal government to get property title to a portion of the land in exchange for extinguishing historic claims. Outside of this one agreement, no Dene land has ever been surrendered. Yet there is not even a small piece of the vast remaining territory that a Dene can use to build a home. Instead, our people must use a foreign system of government to obtain a building permit.

At the same time, it is clear that the Canadian public has always been on the side of some kind of just, equitable recognition and implementation of both aboriginal rights and treaty rights.

Despite the irony of this state of affairs, First Nations were not even party to the drafting of the renewed Constitution of 1982. The governments did agree, however, that First Nations leaders should be invited to participate in subsequent constitutional conferences to identify and define their rights for inclusion in the Canadian Constitution.

That was the first time in their relationship with the Crown that First Nations were consulted about the Constitution, albeit only to a very limited degree. They were, in effect, merely invited to establish and defend their rights. If First Nations had not participated, it is conceivable that non-native governments would have unilaterally identified and defined those rights.

Finding a Genuine Solution

What is it that our people are after? Simply this: We want to sit down across the table from the leaders of this country and come up with a genuine solution that will be acceptable both to indigenous nations and to the people who have come here from elsewhere.

We think there are sufficient land and resources in this country to allow First Nations to retain enough of their original territory where their own institutions can be sovereign.

We don't want to scare Canadians with our terminology. No one is scared in this country by the fact that Ontario or Manitoba can make laws in education and not a single power in the world can do anything about it. They are sovereign in their area of jurisdiction. We, likewise, want to have clear powers over our territories.

Canada is already set up for it, because we have a confederation that lends itself very easily to what our people are asking for. We have the federal government, we have federal powers. We have provinces, we have provincial powers. We have some areas where the two overlap. We could easily have a third list of First Nation powers.

We are prepared to negotiate. But we definitely need enough control over our lives that we can grow, we can flourish, we can prosper. Our people no longer want to be in a situation where you can have a mine right outside your door but the resources from that mine go to somebody else, the employers come from somewhere else, the employees come from somewhere else, the caterers come from somewhere else, and the decision as to *when* that mine is going to be developed is made somewhere else. This kind of development leads to social disruption. The mobile out-of-town workforce, continuing high unemployment, racism, pollution and the disturbance of hunting, fishing and trapping grounds all take their toll when we don't have the power to make decisions affecting our people.

There has to be a peaceful way to share. And if we can't do it in Canada, with the few people we have here, how will any other parts of the world ever be able to settle their situations?

But native people are losing their patience. It's very clear that our people are not going to sit back and take the treatment we have had to take in the past. That much is guaranteed.

The Canadian people must continue to push their governments to sit down with First Nations and negotiate a just and acceptable solution, to reflect what the Canadian polls say Canadian people want. Native people by themselves, it is obvious, are not going to get the Canadian government to take that step.

TIM SCHOULS, JOHN OLTHUIS AND
DIANE ENGELSTAD

THE BASIC DILEMMA: SOVEREIGNTY OR ASSIMILATION

- *The infant mortality rate among native people in Canada (registered Indian population) in 1986 was 17.5 per 1000 live births, compared to 7.9 per 1000 live births for Canada as a whole. ("Registered Indian Population, Infant Mortality Rates," Department of Indian and Northern Affairs)*

- Native people in Canada make up 2 percent of the Canadian population, but almost 13 percent of the prison population (Offender Population Profile, *Correctional Services Canada, 1991*)

- *"Statistics show that in some native communities young people are killing themselves at 4 to 5 times the rate in non-native communities."* (Globe and Mail, *May 18, 1992*)

S TATISTICS — ON INCARCERATION, INFANT MORTALITY, teenage suicide, — serve as a preface to virtually every report or story appealing to the Canadian conscience when it comes to "native issues." To hear that there is *more* poverty, *more* death, and *more* violence in the native community than in any other community in Canada has such a familiar ring that our eyes glaze over and our ears wait impatiently for what comes next.

What tends to get obscured by dwelling on the statistics is the conclusion that all the statistics overwhelmingly point out: Canada's 125-year-old policy of trying to integrate native people into mainstream society has been a monumental failure. As the statistics get worse, the Indian Act and the Department of Indian Affairs continue to regulate every facet of life for aboriginal people, as if these institutions had demonstrated their effectiveness despite all evidence to the contrary.

Ever since Christopher Columbus first stumbled across the continent while looking for India, North America's First Nations have been told that Europeans have all the answers. Settlers hoped that sooner or later the aboriginal people would embrace the benefits of Western civilization, to everyone's advantage. Those who cheated and exploited aboriginal people were ultimately assisted by the attitudes of society as a whole.

Despite the statistics and their way of pointing out how far aboriginal Canadians still are from what is now the mainstream majority, the dilemma we face is not about "equal opportunity" for native Canadians. Fundamentally it is about the sovereign right of First Nations people to live and flourish by a *different* set of values. But Canadians do not like to talk about the sovereign right to be different. It is important in Canadian thinking that everyone is *essentially* the same and wants the same things. There is a belief that what everyone wants is a fair share of the economic pie. An important purpose of most of our democratic institutions, in fact, is to guard against some people taking more than their share of that pie.

So how might we respond to people who do not view their place in Canada in terms of pie sharing, but wish instead to stand firm as sovereign nations resolved to determine their own distinct future with Canada?

Non-native Canadians have to face up to their part in the historical process that has amounted to the near "cultural genocide" of First Nations. Most law-abiding Canadians believe they have carved out their own niche by virtue of their own "hard work" or the labours of their ancestors, and find it unthinkable that they are implicated in the historic tragedy. This perception of individual innocence will have to change: *all* non-native Canadians have benefited tremendously from racist policies, from theft of land and from government defaults on solemn treaties. These are the foundations of our wealth. As in all relationships, to acknowledge that this was *wrong* and to *repent* are the first steps towards healing.

We are now at a crossroads, a time when people of the First Nations, through sheer perseverance and strength, are regaining their dignity and are willing to fight for their rightful place. Non-native Canadians have no choice but to decide how to respond as the first peoples of this country increasingly regain control over their destiny. We believe that to respond appropriately, Canadians need to develop an alternative vision to the colonial and patronizing mindset that has brought the suffering and crises we face today. A new vision should create room for First Nations communities to live out of a set of beliefs different from those that govern the mainstream.

HOW DID WE GET WHERE WE ARE?

If newly arrived Europeans had recognized the right of the First Nations to live according to a different set of beliefs, contact between indigenous nations and European newcomers might have had a different outcome. Here is one possible scenario:

Aboriginal peoples retain their land, way of life and political standing as nations. Europeans gain access to land through treaties, and purchase some land outright (a European notion), where the idea of "purchase" is agreeable to the first peoples who call it their home. As time passes, the newcomers and the indigenous peoples influence one another's cultures. There are significant disagreements about borders and other matters where the different cultures clash, just as there were differences and negotiations among the First Nations themselves, and among European nations. The British, French and First Nations coalitions that form have to work out how to live together in conditions of mutual support and respect.

This outcome is based on the recognition of nations as sovereign and on the political integrity of those nations to uphold treaties. The Royal Proclamation of 1763 in fact acknowledged such sovereignty, establishing a process to protect Indian lands and to legally transfer lands with consent from Indian nations. The fact that this process was not upheld, even though the Proclamation was never revoked, has to do with the cultural outlook of the Europeans. Moreover, the assimilation policies that came to define the relationship between native and non-native peoples reflect cultural attitudes that persist today.

Early settlers believed that they were at a more advanced phase of development as a society than the indigenous peoples they met in North America. It simply did not occur to them that societies could be advanced or complex in a different way, despite the fact that settlers not only learned survival skills from the indigenous people, but also borrowed complex political ideas from them. It seemed obvious to the settlers that the "New World" was destined to become another Europe and that clearing the land for farming was an improvement over what had existed before.

This understanding was interwoven with the belief that people unacquainted with the Christian gospel must be godless and therefore evil. Such a premise inspired fear of the "immoral" deeds the native people might inflict on white settlers, as well as missionary zeal to convert the Indians and improve their lives.

It takes no leap of the imagination to recognize the dynamics already at work. Believing themselves to be culturally and morally superior, the settlers could justify individual and corporate actions to "improve" the land and "enlighten" the people. The benefit of getting aboriginal peoples to assimilate was to lessen the threat to European settlers and their way of life. The ability of Canadians to *justify* the innumerable documented acts of injustice against aboriginal peoples, on the grounds that European culture was "superior," is still a major stumbling block for native people seeking justice today.

No doubt there were acts of kindness and genuine care on the part of settlers and missionaries who shared the Christian gospel and other aspects of their life that they thought worth sharing. But this did not lessen the impact of the cultural baggage that accompanied (and compromised) the Christian message and ultimately defined the framework for native–non-native relations. Many Canadians today would still like to see native issues settled once and for all — by having native people embrace European Canadian values.

INDIVIDUALISM: A WAY OF LIFE

A key aspect of the "cultural baggage" that differed radically from the aboriginal worldview was the idea of the primacy of the *individual* in society. According to liberalism, the ideology that dominates political theory and practice in Canada, the individual constitutes the basic starting point of society. The core attribute of the individual is the ability to think and act rationally; rational action is defined as action that fulfils self-interested goals.

The state's role is to protect the individual's right to self-fulfilment. In liberal theory and practice, two basic rights are required by individuals. The first is the right to *freedom* (and thus the protection from the state against any structure that may interfere with the free activity of the individual). Closely related to the right to freedom is the individual right to *equality*. Implicit in this worldview is the idea that persons are essentially the same, intrinsically valuable and capable of rational action when assured of the conditions of freedom and equality. It follows that the only real social restraint is that individuals should not infringe on the self-fulfilment strategies of others. In order to pursue their interests, individuals need to use the earth's resources, which means that economics play a pivotal role in society. Everyone is equally entitled to a share of these resources, in theory at least, and the marketplace provides the means to regulate fair distribution according to "neutral" laws of supply and demand.

Individuals form groups to assist them in their pursuits, but groups possess no independent existence or rights of their own. Being part of a group is strictly a matter of personal choice as a means to self-fulfilment. Not surprisingly, the group given most attention within liberalism is the voluntary association, a coalition of individual interests; other groups, such as families or ethnic groups, are seen as stepping stones to self-fulfilment.

Steeped in liberal ideology, most non-native Canadians find it difficult to recognize these principles of individualism as anything but universal. Who could disagree, for example, that individual persons have intrinsic worth and that their freedom should be protected? Consequently, it is difficult from an individualistic point of view to allow room for *groups*, and especially for legal protection of *group rights*, because they compromise the freedom of the individual in society. To allow the collective rights of a group of individuals to supersede the rights of the individuals themselves is unthinkable.

But is the liberal view correct in assuming that the individual comes before the group? Perhaps group situations are not always freely chosen in the way the liberal worldview describes. For instance, although voluntary organizations are the normative group of liberalism, they do not match many of the groups that we care most about and that are most salient in our lives. Consider families, religious communities, ethnic communities and tribes, for example. Here group situations are determined *for* people. We are born into families, states and tribal communities, through no choice of our own. But it is in the context of groups like these that the most important human endeavours take place. We perceive ourselves from within group realities — as a sister or uncle, a Cree or Québécois, a citizen. In other words, the constraints that groups impose on individuals may not be as dehumanizing as liberals suppose. Indeed, the development of individual personalities, talents and worldviews *depends* upon the groups to which an individual belongs; such groups should be valued and protected.

The argument for group rights begins with the assumption that, though composed of individuals, many groups also possess an irreducible core, something essential to the communal experience. Consequently, groups argue that their right to maintain their structure is distinct from, and therefore not based on, such individual rights as freedom of association and self-determination. Group rights, they argue, are *qualitatively* different. Interestingly, groups emphasize exactly those things that liberals take to be secondary interests: culture, religion, language. These are often at the heart of the "irreducible core" for which groups seek legal protection.

At the heart of aboriginal claims lies the recognition that the identity and well-being of aboriginal nations and their members are inextricably bound together. Consequently, members of aboriginal nations identify themselves in terms of their membership in the nation and gauge their well-being in relation to the well-being of the nation. For aboriginal people, group rights are essential to continuing their very existence as a people. At minimum this involves the right to freedom from extermination, involuntary assimilation and marginalization. Assimilation poses a threat because it eliminates a group's defining characteristics by incorporating the group in the fabric of the majority's identity.

Given the individualistic worldview that permeates Canadian society, it is clear where the idea of assimilation comes from. Individualism discredits all ways of life that insist upon the right of groups to shape the lives of their members. Instead, the individual is primary and should not be curtailed by the "secondary" matters of culture, religion and language. Assimilation stems from the attitudes of cultural superiority — racism is not too strong a term — which assumed that, when given the choice, any rationally minded native person would opt for the European alternative.

INDIVIDUALISM AS POLICY

It made complete sense, from that point of view, for the state and the church to remove native children from their communities to place them in residential schools. The children would be exposed to a new way of life and then be free to choose their own way of life. They would be provided with education just like other Canadian children, which would create "equal opportunity." The further assumption was that, given the opportunity to make a "rational" choice, native individuals away from the pressures of home would naturally choose the Euro-Canadian way of life with its unlimited opportunities. This policy of assimilation — bringing aboriginal Canadians into the mainstream of Canadian life (liberal individualism) — has been the cornerstone of "Indian policy" since Confederation.

The policy was behind the deliberate destruction of buffalo by running them off "buffalo jumps" in the late 1800s, to make way for European settlement. It was behind the outlawing of traditional ceremonies, the creation of reserves and the promotion of permanent communities, the residential school system that tore families apart and the land claim settlements in which individuals were paid cash for forfeiting their rights as aboriginal people. It was also behind the government's bias towards individual welfare payments rather than support for community self-sufficiency.

Assimilation policy is an expression of both racism and genocide. It is racist to view aboriginal life on the land as inferior to the settler farming culture. It is genocide to forcibly remove aboriginal people from their land or stand in the way of their communal development, thus destroying their existence as a people.

History has borne out that assimilation's publicly stated goal of creating greater "equality" between native and non-native peoples is far from being realized. Canadian governments have consistently dealt with native peoples as if they were children and wards of the state. For well over a century the Indian Act and the Department of Indian Affairs and Northern Development — a telling combination of mandates — and its predecessors have overseen virtually every aspect of native life in Canada.

Another, and perhaps more important reason why the "equality" rhetoric has failed is that aboriginal Canadians have consistently rejected liberal individualism as a way of life. The refusal to assimilate — both conscious and unconscious — has cost them dearly, as poverty and other statistics bear witness. But to have embraced the Western way of life and its definitions of value would have jeopardized what is distinctive about aboriginal values, culture and identity. Despite the incredible pressure to assimilate as individuals, aboriginal Canadians have held on to their identity as members of nations with historic rights, and distinct values and traditions.

ASSIMILATION AND THE WHITE PAPER OF 1969

The core differences between the native stance and government policy were most clearly exposed in 1969 when the Trudeau government unveiled its White Paper proposing a revamped Indian policy. The report recognized that government policies to date had been seriously flawed. The stringent controls and isolation had hindered the natural process of assimilation and had instead created a dependency by Indian communities on government assistance. Paternalistic administration and distinct legal status had denied Indians liberty and equality, and had caused them to be "inward" looking, the White Paper argued. The government accused itself of driving artificial wedges between natives and mainstream society, thereby causing unnecessary conditions of Indian apathy and poverty.

The obvious alternative in the minds of government officials was a new policy based on the principle of individual equality, leading to full and equal participation by aboriginal people in mainstream Canadian society. The proposed policy spelled out the mechanisms that would dismantle special Indian status provisions. The White Paper ignored all calls for group recognition and rights. The government was convinced that the focus by native groups on their ethnicity was a negative response to their sense of exclusion, which could be better addressed through "equality" and "liberty."

The government was not quite prepared for the strong negative reaction to what it had considered a thoroughly rational and perhaps self-evident approach. Diverse aboriginal nations and associations across the country united to oppose the White Paper, and a year later the official native response was presented before a full Cabinet in the form of a document entitled *Citizens Plus*. It categorically rejected the White Paper on the basis that it threatened the cultural survival of Indians as a distinct Canadian community.

Central to the native position in *Citizens Plus* was the assumption that "Indianness" cannot be reduced to an individual or private quality as the White Paper suggested. "Indianness" can only be expressed within a communally shared horizon of meaning. Further, *Citizens Plus* challenged the idea that "isolation" and "discrimination" (special rights for aboriginal people) were the cause of poverty in native communities. Rather, the document charged, the paternalistic and improper manner in which government historically administered aboriginal rights had done the most damage. Conscientious commitment by government to live up to its treaty obligations would have assisted in maintaining healthy, vibrant communities. Indian land would have been protected; hunting, fishing and trapping rights would have been maintained; and health care, educational facilities and economic development would have been provided. As it was, the federal government had neglected its duties and had thus contributed to Indian poverty.

Similarly, although the Indian Act could have been a useful mechanism to define the relationship between Indians and the rest of Canadian society, it instead conferred sweeping powers on the Indian Affairs Branch to regulate the lives of aboriginal people, frustrating attempts at self-government and eroding personal responsibility. The White Paper, native leaders charged, was another attempt by government to avoid its responsibilities.

The government withdrew its White Paper and admitted it had failed to address the problems faced by native Canadians. Trudeau acknowledged that a preoccupation with theoretical (liberal) principles contributed to the policy's inappropriateness.

ASSIMILATION AFTER THE WHITE PAPER

It was less than thirteen years later that the Constitution Act 1982 acknowledged aboriginal rights. Section 35 reads, "The existing aboriginal and treaty rights of the aboriginal peoples of Canada are hereby recognized and affirmed." The recognition was in large part due to the strengthened Indian lobby; it also reflected a considerable change in mainstream thinking about aboriginal rights since the White Paper. But while the thinking has changed, so that today the concept of self-government occupies centre-stage in the political discussion of aboriginal rights, fundamental differences between the mainstream individualistic orientation and the group rights orientation of First Nations continue to plague the process.

Four constitutional conferences, held in order to interpret the meaning of section 35, could come to no conclusion that satisfied both government and First Nations representatives at the table. First Nations argued that "existing" referred to their *inherent* right to self-government (bestowed by the Creator and practised long before European settlement) and to all lands *not* specifically surrendered by First Nations through treaty arrangements. Governments have traditionally argued that "existing" refers to those rights determined and accorded by the treaty claims negotiations process.

In claims negotiations, First Nations seek *recognition* and *implementation* of rights to their ancestral lands, while governments have sought to *extinguish* rights, offering economic benefits in return. First Nations claim to continue to negotiate as legitimate sovereign political entities, in the tradition of the Royal Proclamation of 1763, which formalized relations between the British Crown and aboriginal nations. Self-government, they argue, would not be *granted* but *restored*. Government negotiators, on the other hand, have generally viewed the current constitution of Canadian federalism — power divided between federal and provincial governments — as non-negotiable. "Self-government" has therefore been limited to authority *delegated* to aboriginal communities by federal or provincial governments. "Self-government" in those terms is simply the democratic right of all Canadians to participate fully in the political decisions that affect them, a right native Canadians have not enjoyed in the past.

Government and native interpretations of "culture" also differ dramatically. Today the government emphasis on "multi-culturalism" supports Canadian minorities in maintaining and appreciating their cultural heritage. The tendency is still to view the experience of being Indian as a largely personal affair and similar to the experience of Canadians from any cultural minority. Such a distinction between "public" and "private" simply makes no sense within the aboriginal worldview, which emphasizes the integrality and interrelatedness of all things.

The upshot is that assimilation policy is by no means dead. First Nations are still asked to submit to principles alien to their own way of life in order to resolve the ongoing "problem." Government interprets the "problem" as the lack of economic and political equality native people enjoy relative to other Canadians. For First Nations, the "problem" is that those very interpretations, and their political, social and cultural repercussions, threaten the distinct way of life and identity of First Nations.

MAKING ROOM FOR FIRST NATIONS IN CANADIAN SOCIETY

The revival of native culture and the determination to once again flourish as a people have been truly remarkable in the twenty-plus years since the White Paper. The movement is as clear a message as any that First Nations are not clamouring for equality within the mainstream, reasserting instead their distance from mainstream values. Neither are the aspirations of native Canadians unique; around the world in countries claimed by colonial empires, indigenous peoples are gaining momentum in struggles to protect their ways of life. Liberation movements, civil rights movements and aboriginal rights movements have been the hallmark of the latter part of the twentieth century.

This has in turn created a space for non-native Canadians to question the models Canada has used in its dealings with native Canadians over the past hundred years. Like the government that proposed the White Paper, Canadians who see the great poverty in native communities have had to admit, "We haven't done very well."

The stakes are higher for non-native Canadians than they may have been in the past. Till recently, native people have been in a relatively powerless position and have posed no real threat; Canadians believed it was just a matter of time before native Canadians would be absorbed into the mainstream. Now an articulate, resourceful and sometimes militant generation has emerged, continuing the fight for survival with a new sense of urgency. They have nothing to lose and much to gain. A small minority, but one to be reckoned with, has lost patience with governments' broken promises and believes armed resistance is the only option left. Canadians are starting to feel threatened: What would the recognition and implementation of aboriginal rights — or further stalling — mean for *me?* What do *I* have to give up?

As long as Canadians fail to deal with the grievances of First Nations, Canada's calls for justice in other countries, such as South Africa, will ring hollow in the ears of the international community. And as long as justice is denied to First Nations, every other minority group in Canada will also be threatened. Securing a rightful place for aboriginal nations will be the "litmus test" for whether we can generate mutual respect and responsibility among all Canadian citizens and communities. Canada could be a model for other countries struggling with similar problems.

A NEW VISION FOR CANADA

Canada is not ultimately just a collection of individuals making choices for self-fulfilment. It has often been more aptly described as a "community of communities." To get beyond the situation where First Nations and government are talking past each other, government policy needs to acknowledge the formative role these groups play in public and personal life. The fundamental assumption of our society that the individual is primary and requires freedom of choice above all other considerations is not a neutral concept. It is in fact a "way of life" in the same way that the beliefs and values that shape different cultural expressions in the native community are a "way of life." To the same degree, therefore, that liberal values are given privileged, unquestioned status in the making of laws and policies, they also discriminate unjustly against other distinct visions for life and suppress them.

As Canada is home to diverse peoples and cultures — aboriginal, French and English, to mention just three key groups — it is imperative to find new political and legal means to encourage mutual respect and responsibility for the many distinct ways of life that characterize the Canadian "mosaic." To attempt to squeeze all human endeavours and aspirations into the mould of liberal individualism is not only counter-productive and undemocratic, but probably impossible. People can't turn off their cultural or group identity any more than they can turn off who they are.

Respect for diversity leads to difficult political questions, especially, perhaps, for Christians. How do we extend "love" to our "neighbours," politically speaking, regardless of what set of values or beliefs they adhere to? How does a government deal justly with the diversity in its jurisdiction? What constitutes adequate protection of personal and communal freedom?

Justice requires that public space be provided to allow all communities to live according to their convictions. Christians, liberals and others with strong beliefs about how the world operates must be more willing to extend freedom to those with different views. This requires more than allowing people to think as they like. Governments must not set public policy that sanctions some beliefs and discourages others. Resources, for example, should be made as accessible to communities with "different" values as to those that adhere to mainstream values.

Clearly, this is not currently the case in Canada; aboriginal nations still lack the freedom and resources necessary to live creative, responsible lives. It is absolutely essential, for the sake of basic justice, that their unique claims to resources — which will enable them to once again maintain their own social, cultural and economic institutions — be recognized and dealt with.

It is the responsibility of citizens to support governments in the exercise of public justice and to urge governments to return to a proper execution of their tasks when society becomes a source of injustice. To break out of the current deadlock, we all need to acknowledge First Nations as communities with historic rights, legitimate grievances and the right to direct their own future. Further patronizing through the Department of Indian Affairs or piecemeal attempts at extinguishing aboriginal rights through cash settlements neither solve the dilemma nor serve the cause of justice.

Respect for the group rights of aboriginal peoples has powerful implications, however. The Canadian Constitution should recognize aboriginal peoples as a distinct group in Canada, with inherent rights to self-government. They should be treated as bona fide partners in the constitutional process. Progress was made in the 1992 constitutional conferences towards realization of these goals. Governments must now *fully* acknowledge the inherent authority that was never surrendered by First Nations, and on all disputed claims must negotiate on equal terms.

Non-native supporters of aboriginal sovereignty should be wary of government interpretations of First Nations' demands. A generous cash settlement for land claims is usually no alternative to keeping the land itself, and "self-government" with municipal powers is not the same as self-government with jurisdiction over resources, health and education. It is better to listen to First Nations directly.

There is no simple formula for negotiating the form in which all these rights should be implemented. Negotiating terms of the new relationship with First Nations will be similar to the kind of negotiating that must take place between Quebec and the rest of Canada. A settlement for the Innu of Labrador will undoubtedly differ from a settlement for the Six Nations of southern Ontario. Nevertheless, there needs to be a commitment on the part of the government to an adequate fiscal and land base to enable self-sufficiency.

The principle of self-government deserves the support of the Canadian public and federal and provincial governments as the way to restore the self-sufficiency promised by treaties and the Proclamation of 1763. Canada must honour its commitment to recognizing and affirming the existing aboriginal and treaty rights of aboriginal people. If these rights are simply treated as impediments to progress that can be bought out, the Constitution will have little integrity.

Clinging to the idea that native people should and will embrace mainstream values — the assimilation strategy — would cost governments and taxpayers ever-escalating amounts for welfare and other payments, while tensions rise and statistics worsen. The hallmarks of a mature democracy — and of the kind of society most Canadians would ultimately choose — are respect for differences and protection of minority rights. It's time that we as a nation turned from the destructive and counterproductive task of assimilating First Nations and towards the much more rewarding responsibility of creating room for their self-sufficiency. Attaining justice for aboriginal people is vital as a first priority. But successful negotiations go beyond the protection of only native ways of life. They also make room for other minorities in Canada to contribute to the "mosaic" in new and deeper ways.

Moving in this direction requires "repentance," to use biblical terminology — admitting our failures and committing ourselves to a new road. That commitment won't be easy. It may require that we who have benefited from the spoils for so long have to give up something we hold dear — such as access to "Crown land" or parkland — or that we accept new rules about ownership of natural resources. Some non-native (and native) people may lose their jobs as long-standing institutions like the Department of Indian Affairs make way for new ones.

On a more positive note, repentance will lead to a new partnership between the original inhabitants of this country and the immigrants who choose to call this country home.

All of us have a stake in a Canada founded on justice for all its peoples.

STAN MCKAY

CALLING CREATION INTO OUR FAMILY

WE ARE A PEOPLE of the oral tradition, and I recognize some ambivalence about putting our stories and teachings into written form. Our elders say that when our thoughts are put into written form they lose life, especially when we share important learnings and understandings about our relationship to the creation.

But the present urgent need to come together for a healing vision for the earth, "our mother," has led our elders to advise us to share and risk even by writing.

Art Solomon is an Ojibway spiritual elder from Ontario who attended the World Council of Churches meeting on the island of Mauritius in February of 1983. Art wrote this prayer for the diverse group of people of various faith communities who had gathered there to prepare for the WCC's Vancouver general assembly:

Grandfather, look at our brokenness
Now we must put the sanctity of life as the most sacred principle of power, and renounce the awesome might of materialism.
We know that in all creation, only the family of man has strayed from the sacred way.

We know that we are the ones who are divided and we are the ones who must come back together, to worship and walk in a sacred way, that by our affirmation we may heal the earth and heal each other.

Now we must affirm life for all that is living or face death in a final desecration with no reprieve.

We hear the screams of those who die for want of food, and whose humanity is aborted and prevented.

Grandfather, the sacred one, we know that unless we love and have compassion the healing cannot come.

Grandfather, teach us how to heal our brokenness.

It would be possible to say no more than what Art Solomon has shared in the prayer and to allow you to ponder from that prayer alone how simple our spiritual world view is — and how profound.

Those of you who come from a Judaeo-Christian background might find it helpful to view us as an "Old Testament people." We, like the Israelites, come out of an oral tradition that is rooted in the Creator and the creation. We, like Moses, know about the sacredness of the earth and the promise of land. Our creation stories also emphasize the power of the Creator and the goodness of creation. We can relate to the vision of Abraham and the laughter of Sarah. We have dreams like Ezekiel and have known people like Pharaoh. We call ourselves "the people" to reflect our sense of being chosen.

Indigenous spirituality around the world is centred on the notion of our relationship to the whole creation. We call the earth "our mother." The animals are "our brothers and sisters." Even what biologists describe as inanimate, we call our relatives.

This calling of creation into our family is a metaphorical construction that describes the relationship of love and faithfulness between human persons and the creation. Our identity as creatures in the creation cannot be expressed without talking about the rest of creation, since that very identity includes a sense of the interdependence and connectedness of all life.

Our elders have told stories about the destruction of Mother Earth. In their dreams and visions they have known from time immemorial a deep caring and reverence for life. Living in very natural environments, they taught that we are to care for all life or we may die. The elders say: "If you see that the top of the tree is sick, you will know that it is dying. If the trees die, we too will die." The earth is our life. It is to be shared, and we know the Creator intends it for generations yet unborn.

Because we understand that life is a gift, it makes no sense within our native spiritual vision for either us or others to claim ownership of any part of the creation. Our leaders have often described how nonsensical it is to lay claim to the air, the water or the earth because these are related to all life and are shared by all life.

Chief Dan George expressed it this way in a book entitled *My Heart Soars*:

> Of all the teachings we receive, this one is the most important: Nothing belongs to you of what there is. Of what you take, you must share.

The political process that has become known as "land claims," and in which many of our First Nations are involved with the federal and other governments, is devastating to our cultural values. In order to participate in the process, our statements and language are forced to become sterile and technical. Our documents must be written in language suggested by lawyers and understood by judges. The legal jargon we must use contains concepts of ownership that directly contradict our spiritual understanding of life.

As a marginalized people, forced to live on tiny plots of land, we encounter the worldview of the wealthy and powerful in the land claims process and are forced to compromise or die.

Yet we believe that the earth is to be shared, and we continue to challenge faceless corporations to be faithful to their humanity. Even as we are being pushed into the land claims process, we hold on to our heritage and are motivated by a love of the earth — a concern for the survival of the creation. Our Mother

Earth is in a time of pain, and she sustains many thoughtless children.

The vision that moves us in the struggle towards aboriginal sovereignty is integral to our spirituality. The elders speak to us of our need for balance between the physical and spiritual aspects of our being. They would caution our political leaders not to become so caught up in the struggle for power that they compromise the spiritual heritage that shaped our being. The tradition of the vision quest is founded on the knowledge that we are led by the Creator to spiritual truths that shape both our individual and our corporate journeys.

We understand that the Great Spirit moves through all of life, and is the "Cosmic Order." Our view of creation and the Creator is an attempt to unify the worldview of human beings who are interdependent. We are a part of all life and have no need for dogmatic statements, since our spiritual pilgrimage allows for many truths from a variety of experiences and calls us to live in harmony with other communities.

The word "respect" is central to our movement into harmony with other communities. Respecting others means we accept diversity within the unity of the Creator. We can then engage in dialogue in a global community that does not fall back on defensive arguments to protect any one truth. Instead of making dogmatic pronouncements, we can share stories. Instead of just talking, we can listen.

Living on the earth in harmony with the creation, and therefore the Creator, means moving in the rhythm of the creation. It means vibrating to the pulse of life in a natural way without having to "own" the source of the music.

We have developed myths and rituals that remind us of the centrality of the earth in our experience of the truth about the Creator. We seek to integrate life so that there are no boundaries between the secular and the sacred. For us, the Great Spirit is in our daily, earthly concerns about faithful living. Each day we are given is for thanksgiving for the earth. We are to enjoy it and share it in service to others. This is the way to grow in unity and harmony.

The coming of Europeans to the land we used in North

America led to a conflict of understanding that centres on this concept of the ownership of land. The initial misunderstanding is not surprising, since the first immigrants were coming to "take possession" of a "vacant, pagan land." What is surprising — incredibly so — is that this perception continues after five centuries. Equally surprising has been the historic role of the Christian Church in this process of colonization, which was based upon the division of the earth and its degradation into a mere possession.

The colonial process also undermined the culture and the spiritual values of the aboriginal people. Through generations of genocidal oppression, various agencies have attempted to destroy our cultures. Churches played a role in the repression of our spirituality, and some churches continue to attack the teachings of our elders because their members fear our understanding of the Creator.

One of the major factors in the assimilation process was the policy of taking aboriginal children to residential schools — a practice that isolated whole generations of our people from their culture. The various Christian denominations took on this work of destroying our languages and our stories (under contract with the federal government) precisely because they recognized that they were engaged in a spiritual struggle.

During the colonial period and right up to the present day, the dominant society has also succeeded in turning aboriginal communities themselves into part of the problem. As our self-esteem has diminished and we have accepted the values of the dominant culture, we have begun to oppress our own children. We have denied them the spiritual teachings that could prepare them for a life of wholeness. This situation is now changing.

Recently, some aboriginal people asked the United Church of Canada to apologize for denying the values of aboriginal spirituality. In 1986, at its national General Council meeting in Sudbury, Ontario, after much preparation and discussion, the church did make a formal apology. It was a recognition, by that denomination, of its role in spiritual oppression. The moderator of the United Church read the statement:

Long before my people journeyed to this land your people were here, and you received from your elders an understanding of creation, and of the Mystery that surrounds us all that was deep, and rich and to be treasured.

We did not hear you when you shared your vision. In our zeal to tell you of the good news of Jesus Christ we were blind to the value of your spirituality.

We confused Western ways and culture with the depth and breadth and length and height of the gospel of Christ.

We imposed our civilization as a condition for accepting the gospel.

We tried to make you like us and in so doing we helped to destroy the vision that made you what you were. As a result you and we are poorer and the image of the Creator in us is twisted, blurred, and we are not what we are meant by the Great Spirit to be.

We who represent the United Church of Canada ask you to forgive us and to walk together in the spirit of Christ so that our people may be blessed and God's creation healed.

As a native person, I see this apology from a major Christian denomination as a beginning in a process of liberation that will include a renewed confidence in our own spiritual teachings.

The project of rebuilding our culture and spirituality is supported by teachings of humility, sharing, caring and healing. But we will not be able to call the resulting structure a "sovereign spirituality" for aboriginal people, since that would be a contradiction in terms. Our teachings about spirituality focus on the connectedness of the whole creation; the Creator places us in relationship to all that is. The relationship we hold is therefore based on respect, and our spiritual truth is not meant to destroy but to heal. It is a spiritual vision of Shalom that calls for our full participation as aboriginal people in shaping our future.

The historic process has driven us to become dependent on the dominant society for all our needs. We have wakened from a long sleep, and our dream is now focused on gaining independence.

While this is a necessary part of the growth and healing of the aboriginal people, our spiritual teachers tell us we cannot stop with an image of sovereignty that ends when we regain our political power. Our spiritual calling is to continue the process until our pilgrimage brings us to the place of interdependence. This is the time for the many peoples of the earth to acknowledge our family relationship, which includes us all.

Many teachings among the aboriginal nations of North America use the symbol of the circle — the symbol for the inclusive caring community, where individuals are respected and interdependence is recognized. In the natural order of creation, human beings are a part of the whole circle of life. Aboriginal spiritual teachers speak of the re-establishment of the balance between human beings and the whole of creation as a mending of the hoop.

Those of us who are at the same time aboriginal and Christian face a special challenge and a new responsibility. Since the church has been a part of the oppression, we must redefine what it is to be the church. We must also be reunited with the spiritual strength of our aboriginal culture.

We need to know more about what the elders describe as the balance of body, mind and spirit. Perhaps our greatest challenge is to recognize the danger of being caught up in our political struggle to the extent that we lose again our vision for the healing of creation.

GARY POTTS

THE LAND IS THE BOSS: HOW STEWARDSHIP CAN BRING US TOGETHER

M ANY PEOPLE ARE FAMILIAR with the blockades that took place in Temagami, Northern Ontario, in 1988 and 1989 to prevent loggers from clear-cutting one of the last remaining old-growth forests on the continent. But few people understand the conflict between the Teme-Augama Anishnabai of the area and the environmentalists who initiated the first blockade. And many people do not know what the Teme-Augama Anishnabai want.

The Teme-Augama Anishnabai were caught between the timber industry and the environmentalists. The logging companies wanted to create a desert of our motherland (though the loggers themselves just wanted to put food on the table for their families). The environmentalists, on the other hand, wanted to create a zoo of our motherland.

It was a real dilemma for us and highlighted the need for everyone to understand that the land is a living thing in itself. The land grows because of the living things that interact and return to the earth and decay and support new life. Environmentalists need

---

This article is based on a conversation with Diane Engelstad.

to know that you can't freeze land. You can't fence it off and say, "This is the way it's going to be forever." It's just impossible. By doing this you are also depriving yourself of human interaction with non-human life in a way that still allows the land to sustain itself.

At this time, there seems to be no bridging between the environmentalists and the timber industry. The Ministry of Natural Resources has taken it upon itself to do damage control on public relations so that its own credibility to manage the land is not destroyed completely. The government is trying to engage the environmentalists, the industrial users and the indigenous people in a sort of round-table talk.

Unfortunately, the Ministry sees itself as the source of authority that eventually decides what happens to the land. And this is exactly what we are trying to get away from. We are saying: You're not capable. Your institutions are not geared that way. There's a fundamental flaw in your approach. Our basic disagreement with the government, with the environmentalists and with the logging companies centres on where the authority comes from to decide what can be done on the land. They believe it's up to the Ministry of Natural Resources to make the decisions, based on what all the user groups want.

We say the authority comes from the land itself. You assess what the forest needs to sustain itself and be healthy. You may find you can take 10 percent of the trees or game and not interfere with the forest replenishing itself. But if the land can't support anymore, then you lay your chain saw down. You don't use your gun. You find other ways to live. But you don't kill any life on the land. In some areas you may find that five or even ten more generations of trees need to live and die so the earth can replenish itself. Meanwhile, you document how life exists in that area or make other uses of it during that time.

The land is the boss. The Teme-Augama Anishnabai have always had to hold ourselves back from what we could do with the land, for the benefit of the land and the non-human life on the land, because if you destroy the linkages on that land, then you're destroying something that has evolved over thousands of years. How are you going to excuse yourself for doing that? How are you going to replace it?

Once you know what the land can accommodate and you accept that the land is boss, you're at peace with yourselves because you are in harmony with your natural environment. It's understanding that the land is boss that can get us out of all this confrontation between user groups.

In our particular area, we have proposed a "stewardship model" that recognizes the different kinds of land users. According to this model, the Teme-Augama Anishnabai would have stewardship over a particular area, to ensure self-sufficiency for future generations. We are talking about four thousand square miles because that's what we lived on in the past. With some of the new technologies we may not need that much, but we still require a sufficient amount of land.

Then there are the towns, where people who have adopted our motherland live. The towns would be in charge of stewardship there. And in the areas around the towns, there would be shared stewardship.

An elected stewardship council would meet annually to discuss all the demands being made by human beings and would look at the natural life cycles in the motherland area, and then determine what uses can take place. When people come into the stewardship area, they would buy licences from us, to ensure that they conform to the uses that we have determined — uses that would not push the land beyond the limits that we say the land dictates to us.

Development would not take place for development's sake or for a profit margin. It would be a process of nurturing our motherland to ensure that unborn generations have a base from which to grow. That is the hardest part for non-native Canadians to live with. It is difficult for them because it will probably mean lowering their expectations as to how much wealth can be generated from the natural resources.

Making a living would be based on satisfying basic needs of food, housing and clothing. Our area is not suited for farming. It is mostly rock and small pockets of soil, with trees that have commercial value and animals that have commercial value.

Satisfying basic needs would not mean just the harvesting and selling of natural resources. Work would also take place in the area to bring products to a finished form. Products that leave the area would be stamped with the Teme-Augama land logo to identify them. Then we would document how the products were used in other parts of world. It would become part of the record of what this land has given to society.

It is important that people do not just go out and cut a tree down to get a paycheque without an appreciation of what was there before they cut the tree and what that tree gave to the environment. People should also know where the tree ends up and how it is used, and they should consider whether some parts of it can be returned to the land. That way you have a more holistic picture of the impact that your work and the resource are having on the land, before something leaves and after it leaves.

These changes will not bear fruit overnight. We predict it will take about four hundred years before we are really able to assess how our work is going. But in the next thirty years there would be less cutting down of the forest. We would see new experimental uses of the land, new technology developed and a more environmentally sensitive application of technology to the area to ensure that life is sustained.

It would take thirty years just to document the complexity of all the life forms in the waters, in the trees, in the earth and above the earth, so that the public can better understand what stewardship is about.

This plan might be helpful to people in Canada in another way as well. It would help non-native people develop a national identity that is linked more closely to the *land* rather than simply to a constitution.

JOANNE BARNABY

CULTURE AND SOVEREIGNTY

Before aboriginal peoples came into contact with Europeans, their cultural distinctiveness was relative only to other aboriginal peoples. At the time they perceived these differences as great. But after the arrival of the Europeans, it became clear that aboriginal peoples had more in common with each other than they did with Europeans. It is especially the values shared across different aboriginal cultural groups that aboriginal peoples still struggle to maintain today.

Few non-native people appreciate that Canada's institutions have been determined by a distinctive culture. It is easy to assume that the Charter of Rights and Freedoms, for example, and the Canadian justice system are based on "universal" principles rather than cultural beliefs. That is why most non-native Canadians do not demand the assertion of collective rights: Canadians are generally satisfied that their institutions reflect and protect their collective identity. Some people may not be completely satisfied, but they at least accept the general goals of the institutions.

Aboriginal people, on the other hand, are not satisfied with the values inherent in many Canadian institutions and are striving vigorously for the recognition of their collective rights.

This does not mean that aboriginal peoples are unconcerned with individual rights. Promoting, defining and protecting individual rights is a luxury available only to those who are secure in their sense of belonging and who can identify fundamentally with the institutions established to serve them. Aboriginal societies have not had this luxury since Europeans imposed imported institutions on them through colonial rule.

No Wilderness

Two distinct features of aboriginal societies stand out and help to explain why aboriginal people are calling for sovereignty and self-sufficiency.

There is a fundamental difference between native and non-native concepts of "government." Because of the value placed on the freedom and autonomy of individuals, the Dene, for example, had a decision-making system based on consensus. The consensus system relied heavily on individuals' maintaining significant responsibilities for their behaviour and decisions. The role of leader was not to make decisions but was to advise and make suggestions. This advice would provide the basis for group discussion and could be accepted or rejected. Once agreement within the group affected was reached, the decisions were carried out with support by the group as a whole. Many aboriginal people today feel powerless because the dominant system appears to us as one that gives or takes away individual responsibility through the election process.

The relationship of people to the natural environment, and their place in it, is another distinct feature of aboriginal cultures. Our languages reflect our relationship to creation. There is no Dene word equivalent to "wilderness"; anywhere we go on the land is our home. It is a world view that encompasses far more than the need to make a living and use resources effectively. The relationship between Dene and animals is a very spiritual one, based on equality and respect. In fact, the Dene believe that animals are higher beings than people, because they were created first and have taught our people many things that enable us to live in harmony with the natural environment. Animals may choose to give themselves to us depending on our demonstrated respect for them and for each other. We know we will not be successful in future harvests if we waste meat, do not dispose of bones properly, or fail to share with each other.

We have no right to "manage" or manipulate the natural environment. Rather we seek to understand it and live *with* it. The Dene believe that we have a fundamental responsibility as a people to respect what has been given to us by the Creator, including all forms of life, and to ensure that it is there for future generations to enjoy. Since we have been colonized by Euro-Canadians, our ability to fully live up to this responsibility has been taken away. Our ability to remain distinct has been undermined. Yet, we have resisted the pressures to assimilate and to forget our understanding of the world. We believe it is not only for our sake that we must seek recognition and respect to fulfil our responsibilities, but that it is also in the interest of non-aboriginal people to allow it to happen.

Dene elders believe that the way to maintain a respectful relationship to the land is to continue the traditional lifestyle. Living in a permanent community, created by people, invites the need to accumulate material wealth. But being away from communities, exposed to the natural environment, and harvesting renewable resources that are dependent on wise use and conservation, gives one a sense of the human place in creation that is difficult to find through other means. The land teaches us to be humble and respectful in all aspects of life. Relating to wildlife as brothers and sisters who give themselves up for food and clothing creates the profound sense of stewardship our people feel for the natural environment. Living on the land invites a desire to acquire skills, knowledge and understanding about creation. Acquiring material wealth while living on the land becomes burdensome since people need to move frequently.

Continuing the traditional lifestyle, our elders say, is the only way to keep our ability to communicate with animals, to understand ecosystems and to learn to love creation from a young age. To do this in today's context would require a concerted effort from the Dene themselves, and from governments. Without active support, or at least openness to this lifestyle, the necessary land base will eventually be polluted, destroyed or privatized.

Recent statistics are bringing to light what the Dene have maintained all along. In a report produced by the Canadian Arctic Resources Committee and funded by the government of the Northwest Territories, it is conservatively estimated that the Dene, Métis and Inuit population of approximately 30,000 people in the Northwest Territories are producing food that would cost at least $55 million annually to replace. In other words, hunting, fishing and gathering for food, clothing and shelter — harvesting activities — by aboriginal peoples of the North continue to be economically significant. Indeed, the self-sufficiency made possible by these traditional pursuits far surpasses the value of revenue produced strictly by fur sales. Efforts to place an economic value on traditional pursuits have helped to give recognition and fuller support to the traditional economy. The Dene continue to pursue support for the traditional way of life on economic grounds, while at the same time pressing for a land claims settlement and self-government arrangements that will make the traditional economy less vulnerable.

TRADITIONAL LAWS

To become healthy again, aboriginal societies must have some control over the most fundamental influences that shape and define culture. Our distinct values and ways of doing things must be reflected in our institutions. To make changes effectively we need to first understand our own traditions and be able to transmit that information effectively to those in power.

The Dene Cultural Institute, set up by the Dene National Assembly in 1986, recently began to research and document traditional laws and ways of maintaining social harmony. One institution in particular that needs to change, our elders have said, is the current justice system. The primary objective of a justice system, they say, should be to maintain social harmony. In this respect the Euro-Canadian system has failed our people. The elders believe that emphasizing the question of guilt or innocence invites manipulation and deceit, and detracts from dealing with the reality of the problem. They believe that the use of imprisonment as the main strategy for affecting future behaviour is extremely ineffective and exacerbates problems. Taking the responsibilities of problem solving, rehabilitation and reconciliation away from communities contributes further to unacceptable behaviour. An appropriate justice system is one that would build on the strengths of our traditional knowledge and systems, while retaining whatever is positive in the Euro-Canadian justice system.

Dene and other aboriginal groups are also seeking a return to traditional styles of government. In 1989, the Dene Cultural Institute encouraged the territorial government to establish a working group with representation from all of their major departments and from each aboriginal culture in the Northwest Territories. In 1990, this working group was established with a mandate to "assess and report on the program areas within government (Territorial) and NGOs [non-governmental organizations] in which Traditional Knowledge could be potentially used." The working group produced twenty major recommendations that they agreed would lead to substantial changes within the territorial government and that would result in meaningful representation of aboriginal cultures in the public government. Recommendations addressed issues ranging from personnel policy to the formulation of laws and the role of aboriginal elders in government.

HUMAN RIGHTS

As aboriginal peoples, we must be able to establish or re-establish governing institutions that make sense to us. We must also be able to feel confident that our world view is clearly understood by our own children, and that they will know that their culture has value in modern times as it did in the past. We must be able to teach our children appropriate skills and understanding, and control how our children are taught. We must be allowed to recognize and support our elders, to enable them to contribute fully in life when their physical skills diminish. We must be allowed to use natural resources in a traditional manner. We must be allowed to change, and to direct the evolution of our cultures. Then, and only then, will we have achieved the goals of our struggles for aboriginal rights, and met our aspirations as aboriginal peoples. After all, aboriginal rights are only fundamental *human* rights that have yet to be recognized for aboriginal peoples.

But taking these steps towards cultural self-sufficiency is no longer just a question of ensuring aboriginal survival. How many truly believe that the earth can sustain the demands we make on it in our never-ending desire for material wealth? Much of what aboriginal people have to offer, we believe, could be of great value to all cultural groups, including non-native peoples, resident in the North and beyond, as we all try to change directions away from the massive destruction of the environment. The recent push for "sustainable development" is certainly not new to the Dene. Opportunities to learn from traditional governance and justice systems may also provide answers to those frustrated with the inadequacies of current systems. And educational institutions could learn from the teaching methods of our elders.

There was a time when newcomers depended on our people and their skills for survival on our land. The newcomers learned from our ancestors how to locate food, hunt, trap, travel safely and determine where they were. The time has come again to learn from the original peoples of this land. The kind of learning needed now is much more complex than before. It requires people to question fundamental cultural values and views, and to define new goals.

M ICHAEL A SCH

POLITICAL
SELF-SUFFICIENCY

T HE ISSUE OF ABORIGINAL political rights and especially the right
to self-government holds a central place on the political
agenda of aboriginal leaders at all levels. It certainly provided
the focus for discussion at all the First Ministers' Constitutional Conferences on aboriginal rights — and the conferences
failed largely because the parties could not reach any common
agreement on self-government. Now, however, the federal
government, the territorial governments and most provincial
governments seem at last to have recognized the point that
native leaders have been making for years — that "aboriginal
self-government" is an essential and legitimate expression of
their rights.

GOVERNMENT VIEWS OF
SELF-GOVERNMENT

Although we are now remarkably close to acknowledging that
aboriginal self-government is an inherent right, it is valuable

to examine the stumbling blocks this concept has met with over the past several years of negotiations. Governments and aboriginal leaders have defined aboriginal self-government quite differently — with the possible exception of the NDP governments in Ontario and British Columbia. If we examine some of the differences between the two approaches, we will be better able to understand what is at stake in the aboriginal nations' struggles for political self-sufficiency.

The federal and provincial governments have generally agreed that any political powers they might be willing to recognize in aboriginal self-government must ultimately be "contingent." In other words, they must derive from the present constitutional division of powers between the federal and provincial levels. Aboriginal self-government, they have argued, must depend either on authority delegated from presently existing levels of government or on authority provided by Acts of Parliament. It has been much more difficult for governments to support the specific constitutional amendment needed to recognize anything more than such delegated authority.

The key point of such an approach is that aboriginal self-government is considered a creature of the existing provincial and federal governments, which can be changed or modified unilaterally by them. This is, to put it bluntly, a modern expression of a paternalistic colonialism that attempts to keep aboriginal peoples under the ultimate care and control of non-aboriginal peoples.

Furthermore, when governments have discussed areas of jurisdiction, they have generally wanted to make aboriginal self-government parallel to the existing municipal level of government. For example, an aboriginal government might have the power to run a school board on its own lands, but the right to set the curriculum would remain in the hands of the federal government or the provinces.

On the financial side, governments have generally wanted to retain the final say on the amount to be funded to each aboriginal government.

THE VIEW OF FIRST NATIONS' ORGANIZATIONS

Aboriginal leaders, on the other hand, have always said that self-government for their nations is an *inherent* right that flows from the fact that they are the original nations — the first nations — of what is now called Canada. The United Nations has stated that this "right to self-determination" is held by colonized peoples everywhere in the world, and that no successor colonial regime can extinguish that right by unilateral claims to sovereignty over the same territory.

It is a fundamental right, say the aboriginal leaders. It existed before the creation of Canada, and it continues to exist, notwithstanding the fact that Canada is a recognized nation-state. They point to the Canadian Constitution, which, they say, admits this inherent right to self-government in section 35 (1) of the 1982 Constitution Act, where aboriginal rights are said to be "recognized and affirmed." It follows that the self-governments of aboriginal nations cannot be amended or altered without the consent of the nations themselves.

Most aboriginal leaders, from the local to the national level, have clearly asserted that they are prepared to allow their rights to self-government to be expressed within the political framework of Canada. They are not prepared, however, to accept that the existence of their governments and their levels of authority are contingent on the will of Parliament. They have called, instead, for the specific recognition of aboriginal self-government in the Canadian Constitution through the creation of a third order of government that would have sovereignty and autonomy within its own sphere of activity. This new order would be established through negotiations between aboriginal peoples and the federal and provincial governments. Governmental authority for this third level would have to be constitutionally equal to that held by the provinces and the federal governments.

If, for instance, aboriginal leaders wanted self-government to include jurisdiction over education within its lands, that would mean the aboriginal government would have the constitutionally entrenched power to set the curriculum as well as to run its school boards — without interference from the federal or provincial governments.

Funding for this concept of aboriginal self-government would be based on a formula like the federal-provincial formula for transfer payments, which would guarantee certain levels of funding to aboriginal governments and authority over the disposition of those funds. The setting of funding formulae will doubtless require further constitutional negotiations.

GOVERNMENT STRATEGIES

In the past few years, the federal and some provincial governments primarily pursued their own visions for aboriginal self-government through discussions with various Indian band governments. On the issue of band funding, for example, negotiations generally led to bands taking over the administration of existing programs such as education and housing. Since Indian Affairs still set the overall policy, however, the band government has merely functioned as an administrative arm of the federal bureaucracy.

The other important approach has been to recognize legislative authority for aboriginal self-government on reserve lands through an Act of Parliament. One of the more publicized examples of this was the agreement with the Sechelt Band of British Columbia in 1986. Here, negotiations led to federal legislation granting the Sechelt Band government the power to legislate on their lands in matters that range from zoning and land-use planning to the education of band members — even when Sechelt laws are inconsistent with or different from the laws of British Columbia and the federal government.

While this appeared to be a step forward, we should remember that there was still no constitutional protection for the Sechelt self-government. The federal government could unilaterally change the authorizing legislation at any time. Furthermore, an examination of the Act itself indicates that many matters that could have great impact on the Sechelt Band's lands and members were not under the jurisdiction of the new government. For example:

- Section 40 of the Act states: "For greater certainty, the *British Columbia Indian Reserves Minerals Resources Act* . . . as amended from time to time, applies in respect of Sechelt lands." This suggests that governments other than Band governments could pass legislation on development of mineral resources on Sechelt land without their approval.

- Under section 48, "no interest in lands that are 'Sechelt lands,' as defined in the *Sechelt Indian Band Self-Government Act*, may be expropriated under this part without consent of the Governor in Council." In other words, the band's land could be expropriated by a unilateral order of the federal cabinet.

The above strategies have suited the approach to aboriginal self-government that the Canadian governments presented during the constitutional conferences. From their point of view, the approach has had certain attractions. In the first place, since it required neither constitutional amendments nor structural changes in funding, it supported the view that aboriginal self-government is a contingent right. And since it provided a slightly greater degree of aboriginal self-government than has existed under the Indian Act, it allowed governments to tell the general public that "progress" was being made.

Even the most autonomous of aboriginal governments established under the above strategies would be based on legislation that can be unilaterally altered by Parliament. Ultimate control would therefore remain outside the hands of aboriginal peoples. If the aboriginal governments did not perform in a manner acceptable to Parliament, they could be altered or abolished without the consent of the aboriginal peoples affected. As well, governments would be able to argue that there is no need either to address the issue of "inherent rights" or to expand recognition of powers beyond what currently exists in legislation or to entrench aboriginal self-government in the Constitution.

ABORIGINAL SOVEREIGNTY

On the aboriginal side, the goals and objectives have been much more complex. All First Nations with self-governing arrangements provided through the Indian Act know how powerless they have been, since the Minister of Indian Affairs has had supreme legislative authority over everything from band-government decisions to the composition and indeed the very existence of the bands. In such a situation, even the limited reforms proposed through the Sechelt legislation — or the simple transfer of financial administration — were highly attractive to some aboriginal peoples. Others have not felt comfortable accepting those government propositions.

Political self-sufficiency means, at its most basic level, having the ability to set goals and to act on them without seeking permission from others. When looked at in this way, it is clear that Canada has consistently denied political self-sufficiency to aboriginal nations. Every policy Canada has developed, from the explicit statement in the Indian Act that the Minister of Indian Affairs has ultimate control over band government, to the unstated ability to unilaterally change legislation that lies in the background of the Sechelt Act, has worked in favour of paternalism and dependency and against the principle of aboriginal self-sufficiency in the political arena.

Political self-sufficiency for aboriginal peoples in Canada means not only acquiring certain political and economic resources through negotiations with the federal and provincial governments; it also means acquiring these resources in a manner that is free from both the symbols and the reality of dependency.

Many non-native Canadians find the proposition of aboriginal sovereignty threatening, since it calls into doubt the very legitimacy of Canada's occupation of the land within its present boundaries. To deny the proposition, however, is to suggest that aboriginal nations have fewer rights and expectations than any other indigenous peoples whose sovereignty has also been undermined by colonialist expansion.

This point is not hypothetical. The denial of inherent aboriginal sovereignty has not only been the foundation of government policy but seems to be entrenched in the thinking of the Canadian Supreme Court as well. Two cases illustrate this fact.

In December 1989, the Attorney General of Canada, responding in court to the ownership and jurisdiction assertions of the Gitksan-Wet'suwet'en nation in British Columbia (the Delgamuukw case), stated: "Ownership and jurisdiction constitute a claim to sovereignty. If the plaintiffs ever had sovereignty, it was extinguished completely by the assertion of sovereignty by Great Britain." In other words, the attorney general argued that (1) Canada doubts the Gitksan were ever civilized enough to have sovereignty; but that (2) if they did have it, the mere assertion of sovereignty by Great Britain was enough to extinguish it.

This argument, which was upheld by the judge in the case, is absurd because it is founded on the proposition that the aboriginal people of Canada were too primitive at the time of colonization to have sovereignty, or that their sovereignty was so weak, as compared to "civilized" peoples, that the mere presence of the British annulled it.

Secondly, in *R. v. Sparrow*, a case decided in May 1990, the Supreme Court asserted: " . . . While British policy towards the native population was based on respect for their right to occupy their traditional lands . . . there was from the outset never any doubt that sovereignty and legislative power, and indeed the underlying title, to such lands [was] vested in the Crown." The basis for this view is founded in the international legal principle that, where a land is uninhabited, the first settler obtains sovereignty. To speak of Canada as uninhabited when the Europeans arrived is to suggest that the original peoples of Canada were inherently inferior — not even human. I expect that most Canadians would find this suggestion abhorrent. Furthermore, it is certain that the continued suppression of rights contained within this proposition can only lead to continued conflict with aboriginal nations.

That is why we need to consider what it might mean to accept the alternative proposition — that aboriginal nations have an *inherent* right to self-government.

I believe that we should not be afraid of accepting such a proposition. As I hear it, aboriginal nations are not arguing for non-native people to leave Canada. By and large, they are calling upon non-native people to accept the concept of "sharing" in the political relationship.

It is helpful to think about what "sharing" political power with legitimate national ethnic minorities might mean for world peace. There are very few states in the world without minority national populations that have legitimate rights to self-determination. Up to now, most states have suppressed these rights, and this has led to struggles by the minority peoples against the states within which they find themselves.

The Constitution Act 1867 proposed something different in dealing with the French fact. It provided some basis for accommodation of that cultural minority, albeit in a tentative and circumscribed form. This approach met with only limited success and we are now at a critical juncture where we can reject this approach or build on it. Choosing to build on it means finding alternatives that achieve peace and dignity for nations who are minorities within recognized nation-states. By undertaking this process, we will make a contribution not only to peace and harmony within Canada, but also to the wider world.

In short, we are in a particularly fortunate position. Not only do we have the beginnings of a tradition of sharing, but we are also living with aboriginal peoples who have a long history of constructing political arrangements based on sharing power — and who are prepared to help resolve the political dilemma we now face within the context of that history.

BERNICE HAMMERSMITH

ABORIGINAL WOMEN
AND SELF-GOVERNMENT

THE PLACE OF WOMEN in aboriginal organizations gained national attention in April 1992, during meetings of the Congress of Aboriginal People and the Constitution in Ottawa. Native Women of Canada (NWC) argued that women are excluded from native organizations, and that the existing power structures and process do not encourage women's participation. They said they wanted a seat at the Constitutional table, and they wanted the Canadian Charter of Rights to be put into any deal made on self-government.

NWC is an umbrella group that includes status and non-status Indian women and Métis women, and representatives of provincial native women's groups. (Inuit women have their own organization.) NWC aims to give expression to the voice of all native women, who, the group says, do not see a place for themselves in their own nations. NWC argues that native women belong to largely dysfunctional nations in which justice and equity are practically non-existent.

I believe all this to be true. Native women belong to aboriginal nations that have been shaped for three or four generations by the paternalistic provisions of the Indian Act. Or, if they are Métis women, they have no rights or legal provisions whatsoever; the Métis are truly a forgotten people. In my view, however, giving women a seat at the Constitutional table with government representatives and other national native government representatives will not help us in the long run.

ROOTS OF THE PROBLEMS

I come from Beaver River, a small Cree Métis settlement in northern Saskatchewan across the lake from Ile à la Crosse. I did not start school or learn English until later in life. Beaver River was a community of relatives, based on three or four extended families. The whole community has since been moved to Ile à la Crosse.

When I was twenty years old, I helped my community organize a takeover of the local church-affiliated school. I had come to see that the church had made my community a dysfunctional place. The members of the school board were all non-native, and none of their children went to the school. After the successful takeover of the school, the community was able to determine the curriculum, look after the finances and set policies for our people. This is still the only school in northern Saskatchewan that is controlled by the local native community.

I did this because I was witnessing the effects of cultural genocide in my own lifetime. I had seen a whole community go from self-sufficiency to welfare dependence. I said, "Don't you know that you are being caught up in a system?" But a lot of people felt powerless to stop the process. My father had warned me that this would happen to our people if we did not help ourselves. My parents taught me to work at changing the situation of my people.

The elders are the only link to the stories from the grandparents and the great grandparents. They provide us with a vital connection to a time when we were a proud people. They don't get involved in a heated way as the rest of us do when we are in the thick of the struggle. The elders have time and perspective to reflect on various concerns, to think about consequences. Their advice is always fair and valuable because it gives us glimpses of the past. We do not always want to go back to the past, but we do need to reflect on our own history and find the self-esteem we once had.

In some of our communities women have to deal with a variety of poverty-rooted problems on a day-to-day basis: no money, no food, no shelter. These women are so busy trying to survive that they don't have a chance to talk about their problems, other than to say they are being treated badly. When you are among the troops on the front line, you don't have the luxury of being able to run to the back room to strategize. You can't see which way the battle is going.

One of the main causes of these problems is the treatment of native people who were sent to residential schools two and three generations ago. They were not dealt with in a good way, and now we see several generations of dysfunctional people. That is why there is not much motivation to get an education: school has never been a good place for native people. We lose a lot of our children from the educational system in grade eight or nine or even earlier. They're always pointed to as the problem; they never think of themselves as the solution. And that is how they grow up.

But some have made it through that educational system. We are now seeing a second or third generation — a select few — who have been through the system and have become part of an elected Indian political elite. They know what the game is, so they play that game. And the federal government takes advantage of this. It only recognizes certain people as spokespersons — those who are elected and have adapted to a system the government has concocted and imposed upon us. For Métis people, it is municipal governments. For status Indians, it is band councils. When you ask the band councils, the chiefs or the mayors to change something, they first have to get permission from the people who give them the funding.

The leaders in our communities are paid leaders. This was not traditionally the case in aboriginal societies, and the elders remind us of that. In the past you fixed or changed things because it was your role or duty, not because you were paid. Now money becomes the bigger issue; it's how we trade and make a living. The result is nepotism, which our political leaders have learned very well from the wider governments.

Ironically, it is now our own native politicians and bureaucrats who tell us there is not enough money, just as the Indian Affairs officials used to. The reality is that they are employed by the Department of Indian Affairs. They have become the Indian elite, delivering the government's message that aboriginal people won't be able (or allowed) to change things. Many of the aboriginal leaders have not gone beyond the abuses they suffered as children and have instead become the abusers in their positions of authority. Although there is some value in having our own people working in the government, they have little or no control over the government policies they help to implement. I for one would rather that the abuser was different from me than that it hire my own brother to abuse me.

Women and Aboriginal Sovereignty

The vast majority of aboriginal women are not yet paid by the system; they have no connection to it. As a result, when the women speak out about things that aren't working, they jeopardize the harmony between the chief and the funder, or the band council and the funder. Women become a threat to the system.

Native Women of Canada is right about the problems women are up against in the face of the current dysfunctional male Indian elite. But the opportunity for them to make a place for themselves is back in their own nations, no matter how evil they think the situation may be. It is only by dealing with real concerns at the local level that we will get back to the original values of our nations. This is far from relegating women to the kitchens. Rather it is to elevate the local community and our various nations as the most crucial place for action and change.

NWC was asking for "equal representation." Some of us see this as double representation, since women already have a voice in their respective nations, at least in theory. It is here that they must exercise their influence and, starting at the grass-roots level, encourage leadership and action among women.

The appropriate response to the problem NWC has identified is not to run to the federal government for protection. The first step is to make sure that the new leaders are different. We have to create in each of our communities an environment in which the leaders listen to us and are held accountable by restoring the atmosphere of respect and dignity that once flourished in our circles.

This change in attitude has to come from within the nation, not from an external force. We cannot have the governments saying to us: "We recognize your nationhood but we don't like the way women are treated. So we will impose a solution on you." How soon we forget the hard lessons that have taught us that everything imposed upon us from the outside has had a destructive impact. Neither the government nor any other outside force can make it right for us because it is not connected to the workers on the frontline. It would be like saying: "Protect us while we are fighting." That may be acceptable as a stopgap measure, but it is not nation building.

In effect, NWC was suggesting that we go directly to the level of government *most distant* from the problem. In my view, the local communities know better what the problem is, and therefore can create the solutions. If the community identifies problems such as alcoholism, or TB, or education — or a dysfunctional and abusive male elite — its people must try to solve those problems together, within the appropriate context. When the problem is moved by one giant leap to a higher, more distant environment, the solution is by definition an imposed one. Women, men, elders, youth and even the political elite must work together within their own context if lasting, holistic solutions are to be applied effectively.

We need a grass-roots organization of women in the communities who can strategize on how to change the system. They have to be able to say to themselves, "Yes, I can change something," not, "You go and change that for me while I stay here on the front lines." As NWC has said, it was members of the aboriginal nations who created the current problem (with plenty of help from the rest of Canada). That is why Canada should not be asked to solve the problem: the result would be just another version of the Indian Act. The government says it will help us but insists on retaining jurisdiction over land and resources, child welfare, justice, health and education. This is just the continuation of a policy of genocide.

Making Changes

When we as native women's groups approach the male-oriented groups like the Assembly of First Nations (AFN) and the Métis National Council with problems such as poverty, education and health, the response we often get is, "Those are not our problems," or, "We can't listen to you because you have Treaty women in your organization," or, "We can't listen to you because you have Métis women in your organization." In other words, we as women's groups do not represent their constituencies because we represent a wider constituency.

While it is true that the AFN does not adequately represent the perspective of women, or youth, or elders or disabled people right now, it is still part of its mandate to do so. By developing women's organizations within each of our own nations, we would simply be holding aboriginal governments true to their purpose. This way "constituency" ceases to be an issue.

It is my hope that there will always be a place for women's organizations like the NWC to create discomfort for our leaders who are saying they represent us when they are not doing it in a good way. Maybe this kind of pressure is required for change to take place.

The best time to make the required changes is *now* while Canadians are receptive. In the past few years, this country has fallen in love with aboriginal people. It is no longer "politically correct" to be a redneck. I have noticed a decline in racist treatment, at least by the educated public. The ones who are still frightened of us are the ones who do not know us; it is natural to fear what you do not know. This is not to say there is no longer any racism: there is still far too much racism. But it is not publicly tolerated, possibly because "beads and feathers" are romantic images for the general public. Stereotypical images of aboriginal people still remain. The public knows about poverty and dysfunctional lives among aboriginal people. They see it in their cities and communities and on reserves. They know there is a problem and they feel responsible for it — and to some degree, they are. But the problem won't be solved by studying stereotypical images in textbooks or comic books. And you cannot just send in a task force to look at the issue from a broad perspective and make recommendations. You have to go out and touch people. Both native and non-native people have to work at a community level. Change has to happen through shared responsibility for the community.

ROGER TOWNSHEND

SPECIFIC CLAIMS POLICY: TOO LITTLE TOO LATE

FEDERAL GOVERNMENT POLICY distinguishes between two types of native "claims": *comprehensive claims* and *specific claims*. The term *comprehensive claims* refers to those based on aboriginal title, where there has been no treaty. *Specific claims* refers to claims made in situations where an existing treaty has not been fulfilled properly or Indian reserves or moneys have been misappropriated, usually in violation of the Indian Act.

First Nations do not usually make such distinctions themselves. In fact, some First Nations object to the term "claim," which suggests government ownership of something First Nations are "claiming," instead of something that belongs by right to First Nations. "Claims" terminology displays a government perspective and assumption that treaties between First Nations and Canadian governments extinguish aboriginal rights, rather than recognizing and defining them, and that any rights recognized subsequent to the treaty must be based on the treaty itself, or on legislation, rather than on inherent aboriginal rights.

The definition of "specific claims" systematically excludes issues like hunting, fishing and trapping rights, which arise from the implementation of treaties but are not related to specific lands or moneys. Also rejected out of hand by the government until 1991 have been any claims based on governmental actions prior to Confederation.

One of the most common examples of a "specific claim" is the case where terms of a treaty have not been fulfilled — most significantly, a promise to "give" an aboriginal group certain amounts of reserve land. Another example is a land surrender claim, involving land that was set aside as an Indian reserve at one point, but was taken away by unfair or illegal means. Often, not far beneath the surface of both these situations was the assumption that Indians would rapidly vanish as distinct peoples, and thus the amount of land allotted to or retained by them was considered to be of little long-term consequence. Of course, pure greed was also a major factor in many situations.

Almost all native communities for which land has been set aside have some "specific claims" of these types, resulting in an enduring sense of grievance by those First Nations. Naturally enough, First Nations want redress for these historical wrongs and expect that, in compensating for the loss suffered, this redress would be a significant addition to their land or financial resources, enhancing their prospects for self-sufficiency.

The federal government's expectation from the specific claims process, as we shall see, is to bring closure to the historical grievances at the lowest possible cost.

In reality, the specific claims process meets neither of these expectations. It neither adds significantly to the resources of First Nations nor brings any closure to deeply felt grievances.

The very existence of a specific claims process is a relatively recent development. From 1927 until 1951 it was illegal to raise funds to prosecute a native claim. After 1951, it was no longer illegal, but First Nations faced a legal system that was expensive, time-consuming, generally hostile to the kinds of issues that would have to be raised and rather inflexible about which kind of remedy might be awarded. Before the 1970s, any kind of claim a First Nation might somehow bring to the attention of the federal government was dealt with on an ad-hoc basis.

The Supreme Court of Canada's *Calder* decision in 1973 provided the impetus for change. In that case, the Nishga of British Columbia asked the court for a declaration of aboriginal title over their traditional lands. Although they lost on a technicality, the Supreme Court of Canada made it clear that it was prepared to recognize the concept of aboriginal title, a concept whose existence the federal government had consistently denied. Then, under pressure, the federal government formulated and announced a claims policy. In 1982, the policy was reviewed and revised slightly, but it remained fundamentally the same.

SPECIFIC CLAIMS PROCESS

The substance of the policy as it has existed from 1973 to 1991 is as follows:

Upon submission of a claim, the Specific Claims Branch of the Department of Indian Affairs (formerly the Office of Native Claims) reviews it and verifies the documentation. The department then prepares a statement of fact; that is, a statement of what the Specific Claims Branch considers to be "fact," as opposed to historical interpretation. Of course, the Branch's view of the "facts" may not always coincide with the actual facts. (In one known case, the Specific Claims Branch altered a quotation from a scholarly study so that it would be more in accord with it's own interpretation of the facts.)

When complete, the "statement of fact" is sent to the Department of Justice for an opinion as to the legal merits of the claim. Justice staff usually interpret the government's "lawful obligation" very narrowly, rejecting the methods historians usually apply to evidence in reconstructing past events, and requiring something close to a criminal standard of proof "beyond reasonable doubt." This would be an even more stringent standard than a court would use; in civil cases the standard is "balance of probabilities" (the most probable). The Department of Justice also takes a very narrow view of recent jurisprudence, which has contained some very broad and positive statements of principle about native rights. The Department seems to want to restrict application of these cases to situations with identical facts. Also considered are claims which the Department considers "beyond lawful obligation," claims that would be valid except for limitations of actions[1] or other procedural defences.

When the opinion from the Department of Justice is complete, the First Nation in question is informed of the claim's outcome and the reasoning behind the decision in general terms. The actual opinion, however, is considered confidential advice to the government and is not disclosed. The First Nation, on the other hand, has had to disclose its own legal arguments in order to have its claim considered in the first place.

The Justice opinion is then sent to the Minister of Indian Affairs, who in theory makes the final decision as to whether to accept the claim as valid. In practice, the opinion of the Department of Justice lawyer has almost always been conclusive. Thus the First Nation in question has no contact with the person who makes the effective decision about the claim, nor does the First Nation ever see the decision itself. Perhaps the deepest injustice lies in the fact that the representative of the party against whom the claim was made ultimately determines the claim's validity.

If the claim is in fact accepted as valid, "negotiations" begin, in order to determine the appropriate compensation. The basic legal principle of compensation is that the wronged party be placed, as far as money can do it, in the position she or he would have been in had the wrong not occurred. In the case of native land claims, however, the negotiations are determined much more by the amount of money that has been budgeted for the settlement of specific claims. In 1990–91 the amount was set at $15.5 million for all of Canada. In addition, contrary to all principles of economics, the government considers a loss of $100 in 1900 to be satisfied by a present payment of $100. No computation of interest or adjustment for inflation is made. Yet when payments have to be adjusted as a result of money that the Department has paid out, interest is charged.

Another striking feature of the claims process is the extraordinary amount of time it takes — often five and sometimes ten years. The statistics are truly dismal. Between 1973 and 1989, 515 claims were submitted, but only 79 reached the end of the process and only 38 of those resulted in settlements. One commentator has projected that at that rate, it would take four or five centuries just to clear up the present backlog.

The only way out of this process has been to launch a court action, which is frequently impractical for First Nations. They are faced with high costs and the refusal of Indian Affairs to allow funds from the Department to be spent on litigation other than in exceptional cases. Rules of evidence and procedure exclude certain kinds of historical sources, which may be the only information available. And procedural defences, such as limitations of actions and Crown immunity,[2] are available to the federal government.

CHANGES IN POLICY

Since its introduction in 1973, the claims policy has been severely criticized by virtually all First Nations. After the events at Kanesatake (Oka) in the summer of 1990, the federal government finally seemed to realize how deep-rooted the discontent over specific claims could be. Or viewed from a more cynical perspective, perhaps the government had an urgent political need to at least appear to be doing something on the specific claims front. Whatever the motivation, the government announced some changes to the specific claims policy in early 1991. While there is no doubt that these changes are an improvement, it is far from clear that they will result in the kind of fundamental change needed in the specific claims area.

The changes announced in April 1991 included:

1. A "fast-tracking" process for claims of less than $500,000.
2. Increased funding to claimant groups, to the Specific Claims Branch, and to the pool available for settlements.
3. An independent commission to assist in dispute resolution. (This is not an appeal body and has no binding authority; it only has power to make recommendations to the federal Cabinet.)

4. A joint aboriginal-government working group to address unresolved issues concerning the policy.
5. Consideration of pre-Confederation claims.

These changes are clearly an improvement, but many substantial problems remain. The alterations do not represent a new process; they are merely a supplement to the old process. The commission has power only to recommend, so the most fundamental difficulty remains: the federal government is still judging claims against itself. It is a fundamental conflict of interest to be both defendant and judge, and no process with this feature will be fair.

Furthermore, although the commission would presumably be helpful in forcing the government to detail its legal position, the opinion of the Department of Justice regarding the legal merits of the claim will likely remain confidential and will therefore be hard to respond to. Nor is the commission mandated to manage and speed up the process as a whole; that power remains with the federal government.

Except for the removal of the pre-Confederation bar, all substantive parts of the policy remain unchanged, and the commission will be bound by them. There is a possibility that the joint aboriginal-government working group could stimulate changes in the policy itself, but this remains uncertain. So, at least in the short term, matters of treaty implementation that cannot be reduced to specific land or money will not be included, nor will there be any change in the narrow interpretations of law and fact by the Department of Justice, nor in the calculation of compensation, which defies legal and economic principles in its failure to take into account interest and inflation; neither is there any guarantee that these things will change later.

The federal government retains control of the funding it provides to First Nations for claims preparation. No funds are available for historical or treaty research work if such work does not fit the particular parameters of a "specific claim," even if that research is a priority for the First Nation concerned.

Throughout these problems runs the common thread of the conflicting goals of the two parties concerned. The First Nations want redress for historical wrongs, redress that would provide enough resources to significantly increase their ability to be self-sufficient. The federal government wants to make the problem go away at the lowest possible cost. Yet it has failed to realize that a process that appears so unfair will never resolve deeply felt grievances.

The government has also failed to recognize that increased self-sufficiency for First Nations is in the long-term interests of everyone involved. So the process limps along, fulfilling neither of the conflicting goals.

The federal claims process leaves First Nations with only two real alternatives: legal action or direct on-the-ground action. Some of the problems with legal action have already been noted: the expense, procedural pitfalls like limitations of actions and Crown immunity and an inflexible list of the types of compensation possible.[3] Since they are faced with such difficult, frustrating and uncertain recourse through either the claims process or the courts, it is not surprising that some First Nations turn to on-the-ground action.

It was in response to such action at Kanesatake that the latest changes in the claims policy were announced. It remains to be seen whether the changes will be sufficient to prevent future military confrontation with First Nations.

M U R R A Y   A N G U S

COMPREHENSIVE CLAIMS: ONE STEP FORWARD, TWO STEPS BACK

M UCH HAS HAPPENED on the comprehensive claims front since the Conservatives took office in 1984 — far more than anyone would have predicted at the beginning of their term. A major review of claims policy was undertaken, culminating in the landmark *Coolican Report* of 1986, and by the fall of 1989 three agreements-in-principle had been signed involving the largest claims in the country: the Dene/Métis, the Yukon Indians and the Inuit of the Eastern Arctic. After a decade of stalled talks under the Trudeau Liberals, these achievements appeared to signal undeniable progress.

To assess the significance of these events, however, we need to go back to the origins of the process itself and be reminded of what native groups originally sought to achieve through their land claims negotiations. The comprehensive claims process was born in an era when aboriginal people, particularly in

This article has been adapted from *And the Last Shall Be First: Native Policy in an Era of Cutbacks* by Murray Angus (Toronto: NC Press Limited, 1991); reprinted with permission.

northern regions, were threatened with sudden, uncontrolled development pressures. Faced with the prospect of having their lands and communities changed irreparably by the activities of oil companies, with no guaranteed benefits in return, aboriginal people began to organize to assert their rights.

The government's first response was to deny that aboriginal people had any rights. On the basis of this assumption (which it was confident the courts would support), Ottawa backed the plans of developers as if aboriginal people didn't exist. When public sympathy for the native position began to emerge in the early 1970s, the government modified its position slightly and expressed a willingness to discuss the concerns of native people, if only for appearances. Its motives remained entirely political; assuming it still held all the legal cards, it felt under no obligation to give in to any native demands.

Ottawa's strategy was thoroughly undermined when the Supreme Court of Canada rendered its historic *Calder* decision in January 1973. In this decision, the Court ruled unanimously that aboriginal peoples who had never signed treaties could, in theory, retain aboriginal title to the lands they traditionally used and occupied. Such a right could be extinguished only if it had been surrendered in a treaty or superseded by other laws passed by the Crown.

This decision had momentous implications for the struggles taking place in the North. Since the majority of native people north of the 60th parallel had never signed treaties,[1] Inuit, Dene and Yukon Indians still retained, potentially at least, a legal right to lands covering one-third of Canada. The possible existence of such rights injected new — and, from the government's point of view, unexpected — uncertainties into the development process. It meant native people had a legal basis from which to challenge the government's jurisdiction over the lands in the North and, by extension, the activities of developers. That the courts had failed to clarify what specific rights were associated with aboriginal title only increased the ambiguity for both government and industry.

Not surprisingly, native groups in the North gained enormous political leverage from the *Calder* decision. At the time, industry was moving ahead rapidly with plans for megaproject developments. Ottawa was assisting it with generous tax write-offs and publicly financed infrastructure such as the Mackenzie Valley Highway. The legal wild card dealt to native people by the courts threw the whole question of authority over the North into the air. Suddenly, the government had its own reasons for wanting to talk.

Six months after the Supreme Court ruling, the Liberal government brought out a new policy for dealing with the rights (whatever they might be) of aboriginal people who had never signed treaties. While it confirmed the government's new-found willingness to engage in dialogue, it also demonstrated Ottawa's determination to control the outcome of any negotiations. The policy, announced on August 3, 1973, was not intended to facilitate any sharing of power with native people, particularly over development. Instead, it established a process for negotiations that would culminate in the payment of large amounts of cash to native people in exchange for the extinguishment of whatever aboriginal rights they might possess. This offer represented little more than an updated version of the treaties signed one hundred years before on the Prairies; it was an approach designed to buy native people off and to eliminate their ability to intrude on the decision-making process, especially as it related to impending resource development on their land.

No doubt aware of the experience of other native people in the south who had been "bought off" through a similar approach in the past, native people in the North were quick to reject the government's simplistic "cash for land" approach. They recognized that cash alone would not protect their long-term interests. Their lands and communities were being threatened by a development process orchestrated by outsiders for the benefit of outsiders; if their cultures were to survive, they would have to secure some degree of ongoing control over the lands upon which they depended.

Their strategy for obtaining that control was to include political rights on the land claims agenda. Only by the recognition of their political rights, it was argued, could they hope to control the nature, pace and location of development on their lands.

Only by acquiring political rights could they be assured that decisions would be made in the interests of northerners versus southerners, and especially in the interests of natives versus non-natives. "No pipeline before a land claims settlement" became the slogan used by all northern aboriginal groups to convey their determination to secure those rights before any development took place. Although the Inuit pursued this strategy through their Nunavut proposal in 1976, it was the Dene Nation that expressed the demand for political rights with the greatest eloquence and force. The Dene Declaration of 1975 was the landmark event in the evolution of native politics in the North. It identified the Dene as a "nation" and declared "self-determination" to be the objective.

The government was having none of it. Federal politicians went out of their way to ridicule the Dene Declaration, calling it "gobbledegook." Federal negotiators were prohibited from discussing political rights at anything beyond a local level, thereby denying the Dene effective power over their region. But native groups were quick to recognize the limitations of the government response. They realized that unless they gained some degree of ongoing control over their regional economies, they could never exercise control over developments that would have the greatest impacts on their communities and culture. Despite government attempts to bully them (by labelling their demands "separatist" and "Marxist" and by cutting funding at strategic moments), the native groups refused to back down. The result was a stalemate in negotiations which lasted throughout the rest of the 1970s.

By the early 1980s, the strategies of the native groups began to shift. This was a result of political and economic changes that had been occurring in the North. The issues in the early 1970s were, What kind of development should take place in the North? and even more important, Who was going to decide? By the early 1980s, these questions had been resolved unilaterally by the federal government. While native people held out at the claims table for the political rights needed to control development, the federal government had gone ahead and implemented the model of development it preferred from the outset. This model involved giving massive public subsidies to large private corporations to enable them to extract resources for export. It offered few lasting benefits to the North or its peoples.

While none of the proposed energy megaprojects ever got off the ground, Ottawa did proceed to bankroll the oil and gas industry with billions of dollars of subsidies and write-offs throughout the 1970s, and put in place the infrastructure to support large-scale resource exploitation in the Mackenzie Valley and the Beaufort Sea. The issues of whether this type of activity would be allowed, and on whose terms, were decided by default, and the inability of the native groups to stop development pending the resolution of their claims had become increasingly apparent. The only attempt by a native group to challenge the government's development activities in court during this time — made by the Inuit of Baker Lake in 1979 — proved singularly unsuccessful in meeting its primary objective. The federal court confirmed that the Inuit had aboriginal title to the lands in question, but insisted that this did not give them the right to stop uranium companies from exploring on their land.

Once it became clear that development was going to happen even in the absence of a settlement, pressure began to grow at the community level to resolve claims and to "catch a ride" on the development that was occurring. This was especially the case in the areas that were under the greatest pressure from development.

In 1976, the Inuvialuit of the Beaufort Sea region, represented by the Committee for Original Peoples' Entitlement (COPE), decided they could not wait for the larger Inuit claims to be settled. They opted to pursue their own negotiations, which culminated in a settlement in 1984. The settlement did not challenge the basic parameters of the government's land claims policy, relying on advisory boards rather than political rights to implement changes. Development pressure also contributed to the decision by the Dene in 1980 to support the construction of the Norman Wells pipeline, even though no progress had been made on their claims. "No pipeline before a land claims settlement" was clearly a strategy that had not worked.

One factor that allowed native groups to gradually concede

the issue of political rights at the land claims table was the emergence in 1979 of a native majority in the Legislative Assembly of the Northwest Territories. This trend gave rise to the hope that the territorial government could provide an alternate vehicle by which natives might obtain, if not political rights as interpreted by the aboriginal community, at least political control through the existing electoral process. The Inuit carried this strategy furthest. In 1979, they made a decision to separate their quest for political rights from the land claims process and to pursue political control through the creation of a new territory called Nunavut, where Inuit would make up the vast majority of the voting population.

With political rights gone from the land claims table, negotiations progressed more quickly. This did not mean that native groups were any more willing to accept the government's original cash-for-land offer, however. Led by the Inuit, they pushed for a strong role in the management of lands and resources at the regulatory level. The government had no problem with the creation of innumerable "advisory" boards (it had set up dozens in the COPE settlement), but the Inuit and Dene wanted more: an equal say in regulatory bodies that would have actual decision-making powers over land-use planning, water management and the impact review process relating to development projects. If the central struggle of the 1970s was over political rights, the equivalent struggle of the 1980s was over management rights.

It was against this backdrop that the Conservatives came to power in 1984. While most observers predicted a "get tough" approach to claims from the new government, its first moves proved surprising. Perhaps the greatest surprise was the appointment of David Crombie as Minister of the Department of Indian Affairs and Northern Development (DIAND). Crombie had been a popular mayor of Toronto in the 1970s but, while successful as a politician, he had virtually no background in native issues. What he brought to the job was a populist style, an enthusiastic attitude and a relatively open mind. He also surrounded himself with a team of advisors experienced in, and sympathetic to, native rights issues.

One of Crombie's first acts as minister was to set up a task force to review the government's comprehensive land claims policy, in the hope of overcoming the inertia that had characterized the process during the Liberal years. To conduct the review, Crombie drew once again upon experts who were knowledgeable about, and even sympathetic to, the native cause.

The task force's report — *Living Treaties: Lasting Agreements,* also known as the Coolican Report — was sweeping in scope. It called for not just a new policy on comprehensive claims, but an entirely "new relationship" between the government and native people in Canada. Comprehensive claims, it said, should not be approached as once-and-for-all "cash-for-land" transactions, but rather as "a first step" toward "the building of self-sufficient aboriginal communities." It argued, "The new policy should encourage aboriginal communities to become not only economically self-sufficient but also to establish political and social institutions that will allow them to become self-governing." It called for agreements that would be "living" documents and "flexible" over time, "to allow for growth and to meet the changing needs of aboriginal communities and Canadian societies." It argued strongly that native people should "share in the financial rewards of development on their traditional territories," because "political power is meaningless without the backing of financial resources." Finally, it stated that native people should not be made to surrender totally their aboriginal rights as a precondition for settlements.

The task force report, not surprisingly, was hailed by many native people and their supporters as visionary. In the months following its release, an intensive lobbying effort was undertaken to build political, bureaucratic and public support for its recommendations. Unfortunately, by this time, the minister who had sponsored the policy review had lost much of his interest in the issue. The complex and seemingly intractable nature of native problems was too much even for David Crombie's populist and enthusiastic approach. There could be no "quick fixes" to native problems, and Crombie increasingly wanted out. Near the midway point in the Conservatives' term, before any new policy recommendations were taken to Cabinet, he got his wish.

The man who replaced Crombie as the new Minister of Indian Affairs and Northern Development was Bill McKnight, a straight-talking farmer from Saskatchewan with no outward interest in, or sympathy for, native concerns. In terms of style, he was Crombie's opposite. He had no interest in mingling with or learning from the people he was supposed to be serving and was more inclined to take direction from his department's bureaucrats. His main concerns were to tighten up the financial administration of his department and to keep native issues out of the headlines.

McKnight had the responsibility for taking recommendations for a new land claims policy to Cabinet. The resulting new policy, announced in December 1986, reflected little of the vision of the Coolican Report. It avoided much of the discussion about the broader goals of comprehensive land claims — to develop self-sufficient, self-governing native communities — and contented itself with a clearer delineation of what would, and would not, be negotiable at the comprehensive claims table in the future.

This greater clarity had potential to be a positive step. The old policy was, in fact, hampered by vagueness, resulting in federal negotiators running back to Cabinet for directions every time an innovative proposal was placed before them. While the new policy eliminated this vagueness to a large degree, it often did so in a regressive way.

On the positive side, the new policy opened the door for the first time to the negotiations of matters long sought by native groups: joint decision making over lands and resources, resource revenue sharing and rights to the offshore. The government's restrictive application of the new policy, however, has meant that native groups have sometimes been left worse off than before.

In terms of resource revenue sharing, the new policy continues to reflect the view that claims settlements are really only a mechanism for "buying native people out." Instead of recognizing that native people have a legitimate, ongoing right to benefit from resources on or under their lands, the new policy imposes limits on how much they might benefit from resource revenues. The only new thing Ottawa is willing to negotiate is the formula by which such benefits can be capped (by fixed dollar amount, by time frame or by a reduced royalty percentage). At the same time, native groups are being told that any gains derived from resource revenues will ultimately have to be taken from other parts of the settlement package, such as compensation. The new policy is not designed to provide native people with a greater financial base; it merely expands the range of options by which they can be "bought off."

Regarding the potential arrangements for jointly managing land and resources, the story is the same. While the new policy recognizes "aboriginal *interests* in relation to environmental concerns, particularly as those concerns relate to wildlife management and the use of water and land" (emphasis added), it backs away from an acknowledgment of any *rights*. At the same time, it reaffirms the government's determination to "protect the interests of all users, to ensure resource conservation . . . and to manage renewable resources within its jurisdiction." To this end, it states clearly that land claims settlements "will not result in the establishment of joint-management boards to manage subsurface and subsea resources." In the case of the Inuit, who had succeeded in negotiating such joint management bodies under the old policy (however tentatively), this new policy represents nothing more than a giant step backwards.

While Ottawa is now willing to consider at least a superficial native role in the management of lands and resources, it still prefers such a role to remain "advisory," with the government retaining the final say over development. The only new twist is that it is willing to negotiate a guaranteed role for native people on any public bodies dealing with land and resource issues. The downside of this offer is that the eventual powers of such bodies will be decided by the government. As long as this remains the case, it is unlikely that such boards will ever be given any independent authority or regulatory teeth.

The new policy also brought clarity as to what will not be negotiated at the claims table. Native groups used the vagueness of the old policy to advantage by loading the agenda with every conceivable item they could think of, in the hope of making claims settlements the basis for a broad "social contract" between themselves and other Canadians. The new policy has brought an end to this hope. The Conservatives had made it explicit that comprehensive claims are primarily about land and not much else. They have rejected the negotiation of language rights, health and social provisions or broadcasting rights under the new policy. More pointedly, they have refused to negotiate anything that might constitute a new and ongoing program at the claims table. Tragically, this includes hunter income-support programs, which have proven cost-efficient and culturally reinforcing in the areas where they have been established (such as James Bay and northern Quebec).

The government's unwillingness to consider any new ongoing rights or jurisdictions is another indication of its continuing "buy-out" attitude toward claims. Despite the Coolican Report's call for settlements that will be "living agreements" and "flexible" over time, the government continues to hold to the view that claims are "once-and-for-all" transactions, with fixed and preferably limited costs. The policy of avoiding any new ongoing program expenditures as a result of claims settlements is another example of the government's determination to limit its long-term financial obligations to native people in Canada.

The current Tory policy can be said to represent "one step forward and two steps back" for native people attempting to negotiate comprehensive land claims settlements. The Conservatives have succeeded in eliminating much of the ambiguity of the previous Liberal policy, but the result, with a few notable exceptions, has been to narrow the basis on which claims can be negotiated. This narrowing can be attributed to two factors: Ottawa's determination to retain public control over resource development at the regulatory and political levels and its determination to avoid any long-term, open-ended financial commitments to native people.

Looking back over the last twenty years, Ottawa has been successful in implementing much of its original agenda on the claims front. In the North, it put into place the model of development it preferred from the outset, especially as it pertains to the resource development sector. Through successive land claims policies, it prevented native people from intruding on its exclusive control over the development process — at least on the basis of their aboriginal rights. It achieved the latter by successfully preventing native groups from negotiating political rights at the land claims table throughout the 1970s and by resisting attempts to negotiate a meaningful share of management responsibilities at the regulatory level in the 1980s.

Events in the North will ultimately decide the future of Ottawa's comprehensive land claims policy. The Dene Nation signed an agreement-in-principle in 1989 with Ottawa, but disagreements over extinguishment led to a subsequent breakdown in talks. Two of the Dene groups that were willing to accept the extinguishment clause have since negotiated their own separate agreements. Those that refused to accept extinguishment as a condition for settling have had their funds cut off.

The Inuit claim in the eastern Arctic may be one which ultimately "makes or breaks" Ottawa's policy. The Inuit have spent ten years negotiating an agreement that will lead to the creation of a new territory in which they will be the majority. They will also secure joint-management rights to the land and the resources of the region. An Inuit vote on the package is scheduled for late 1992. If it is approved, Ottawa will have secured the biggest claim of all — and will have done so under the existing policy. If the claim is accepted, Ottawa will have little incentive to change its policy for any other groups, knowing that it worked with the biggest one. If the Inuit reject the package, however, it could render the existing policy untenable, and Ottawa could be forced back to the drawing board.

P ATRICK   M ACKLEM   AND
R OGER   T OWNSHEND

RESORTING TO COURT: CAN THE JUDICIARY DELIVER JUSTICE FOR FIRST NATIONS?

A S A STRATEGY for protecting aboriginal rights, resorting to the Canadian courtroom is fraught with risk. Litigation is expensive and time-consuming, and results are hard to predict. European-Canadian legal concepts are usually foreign to aboriginal ways of resolving disputes. And, backed by the arm of the state, judicial decisions that conflict with aboriginal visions of social justice have a way of stubbornly entrenching themselves in the legal landscape. It is generally true of all litigation, but especially true of First Nations claims, that other means of settling disputes, like negotiation, are vastly preferable to resorting to the courtroom, and are more likely to yield an outcome acceptable to all parties involved.

But is the judiciary valuable when all other avenues have been exhausted? Can courts assist in advancing the cause of aboriginal rights and self-determination?

It is true that the courts have often functioned to maintain the status quo, to the severe detriment of First Nations. Many legal principles generated by judicial decision making in the past continue to cast a long shadow over the present. Often these principles were and are supported by a selective use of rhetoric about either the similarities or differences between aboriginal and non-aboriginal peoples. Difference *and* similarity have been denied when the suggestion of either would lead to questioning basic European-Canadian concepts concerning the nature of property, contract, sovereignty and constitutional rights.

However, despite what could be termed a "structural bias" in the law against aboriginal aspirations, judicial decisions in the last twenty years show there is a potential for transformation, and they hint at ways in which the law might be used to advance the cause of aboriginal peoples. The courts have often been more sympathetic to aboriginal hopes than the political forum. In turn, court decisions have prompted a number of policy break-throughs in the political arena in the past twenty years. Yet the question remains as to whether the judiciary can actually deliver justice to First Nations.[1]

THE TRADITIONAL FRAMEWORK

Any discussion of Canadian law dealing with aboriginal rights must begin with *St. Catharines Milling and Lumber Co. v. R.*, decided in 1888.[2] Like many cases of its era, it was decided without aboriginal people being represented legally in the proceedings. The case arose out of a federal-provincial dispute over which government had a right to issue timber licences on lands occupied by the Ojibway Nation. The federal government argued that it had acquired title to the land from the Ojibway by virtue of Treaty Number Three. The province of Ontario argued that it had owned the land prior to Confederation and that Confederation did not alter provincial property holdings. To determine whether the federal government might have obtained title from the Ojibway, it became necessary for the judicary to decide what kind of property rights the First Nation had before treaty. The Privy Council[3] found that the Ojibway rights were "personal and usufructory" (i.e., use-oriented) and did not amount to full ownership of the land. The province therefore held title, and when aboriginal rights were ceded to the federal government by treaty, the province enjoyed full title and possessed the right to issue timber licenses.

St. Catharines Milling assumes that the Crown enjoys sovereignty over, and property rights in, First Nations territory, and simply carves up sovereignty and property rights to accommodate a federal system of government. In making such an assumption about Canadian sovereignty and property rights, the Privy Council referred to American case law on the subject.

One of these American cases, *Johnson* v. *M'Intosh*[4] continues to dominate Canadian law and indicates the interplay of how ideas of similarity and difference were used to the extreme disadvantage of aboriginal peoples.

In *Johnson* v. *M'Intosh*, the United States Supreme Court held that British sovereignty was grounded in international legal principles governing the discovery of new lands: sovereignty is vested in the nation that is the first to discover new lands. The problem to be overcome was that this doctrine applied only to "unoccupied" lands. However, international law at the time provided that occupancy by aboriginal peoples did not, in law, render lands "occupied." Aboriginal forms of social organization, being more holistic and collective, were considered insufficiently civilized to merit legal recognition. Native "difference," in other words, enabled international law and Chief Justice Marshall in *Johnson* v. *M'Intosh* to invoke the principle of discovery to justify European claims of sovereignty over First Nation lands.

Crown property rights to land, however, were justified in *Johnson* v. *M'Intosh* by viewing aboriginal people as *similar* to non-native people. Applying the British theory of landholding, which assumes that the Crown is the original owner of all land and that private property rights are granted by the Crown, the Court said that full ownership of land by aboriginal people would require a grant from the Crown. Since in most cases no such grant had been given to aboriginal people, full ownership rights continued to lie with the Crown. Using this justification, the Crown could do what it liked with the land, including extinguishing aboriginal rights and granting the land to other parties.

The view articulated in *Johnson* v. *M'Intosh* was accepted by the Privy Council in *St. Catharines Milling* without any sustained analysis and has haunted the jurisprudence to this day.

While there are certainly cases more respectful of aboriginal rights, the view that aboriginal rights are dependent on the discretion of the Crown continues to have force. In 1989, the Ontario Court of Appeal took the view that the aboriginal title of the Teme-Augama Anishnabai Nation had been unilaterally extinguished by the Crown.[5] In 1991, the British Columbia Supreme Court held that any sovereignty enjoyed by the Gitksan and Wet'suwet'en peoples in British Columbia was extinguished by the assumption of sovereignty by the imperial Crown, and any aboriginal rights to land were extinguished by colonial enactment.[6]

Intimately tied up with the way aboriginal title has been defined is the idea that the Crown has established itself as a mediator between aboriginal peoples and the non-native public to protect aboriginal interests.[7] Although such a role seems promising, it represents, by definition, a denial of aboriginal self-government. Moreover, this conception of the Crown places the Crown in a potential conflict of interest between its roles of acting in the public interest and of protecting aboriginal interests. It is not hard to imagine which duty usually wins out in practice.

Given the ambivalent and potentially contradictory role of the Crown, judicial interpretations of the treaties become crucial. There are several cases finding that treaties amounted to little more than personal obligations of the governor who signed them,[8] and that treaties are promises that Parliament could not be prevented from breaking if it so chose.[9] Fortunately, 1982 constitutional amendments require the courts to view treaties as constitutional documents, binding upon the legislative authority of the Canadian state.

BREAKTHROUGHS IN THE COURTS

In 1969, the federal government released a "White Paper" announcing a policy that special Indian status be ended and that aboriginal people become integrated into general society.[10] This policy met with immediate and unanimous rejection by the First Nations, and the government had to abandon it as unworkable.

Nevertheless, the sections of the paper that concerned aboriginal title became government policy. "Lawful obligations" — namely, any explicit treaty promises — were to be met, but general aboriginal title claims in those sections of Canada where there had been no treaties were considered too vague to be recognized. Thus, in the early 1970s, contrary to historic British colonial policy and Canadian government practice in the late 1800s and early 1900s, there was no possibility of discussing with the Canadian government arrangements based on aboriginal title.

In this context, the Nishga Nation, on the northwest coast of British Columbia, brought forward a lawsuit asking for a declaration that the Nishga had aboriginal title *(Calder* v. *Attorney General B.C.).* They lost on a technicality, but six Supreme Court judges recognized that there was such a thing as aboriginal title in Canadian law and three of the judges concluded that the aboriginal title of the Nishga still survived.[11]

In response, the federal government abandoned its position and formulated a policy for dealing with such matters. This was the origin of the "comprehensive claims" and "specific claims" policies. Whatever their shortcomings, at least they now exist, and owe their creation to the *Calder* decision.

Another breakthrough in the courts arose in the *Paulette* case.[12] The Dene Nation in the Northwest Territories was trying to negotiate an aboriginal title claim. The federal government resisted their arguments, claiming that Treaties Eight and Eleven extinguished aboriginal title. The Dene then tried to file a caveat in the territorial land registry system, which would have warned any potential buyers of land of their claims, thus making land more difficult to sell.

The question of whether or not the Dene could file a caveat in this way went to court and the trial judge found that there was enough doubt about the validity of the treaties that he would permit a caveat. The Dene lost on a technicality on appeal, but the decision was influential enough that the federal government decided to negotiate with the Dene. This was the beginning of a long period of negotiations that have still not been completed. Again, it was the intervention of the court that made negotiation possible at all.

A similar impetus from the courts took place in connection with northern Quebec. In the early seventies the Quebec government was proceeding with construction of the James Bay hydro-electric project without regard to the rights of the James Bay Cree. The Cree obtained an injunction to halt construction in 1973,[13] and although this decision was quickly reversed by the Quebec Court of Appeal, the threat of a Supreme Court decision in favour of the Cree was sufficient to stimulate a negotiated agreement — the James Bay and Northern Quebec Agreement. However one judges this agreement, the alternative was worse. The Cree were facing the prospect of dams being built without any agreement at all. Without the intervention of the court they would likely have received no compensation.

AMBIGUOUS JUSTICE

What happens if the negotiations stimulated by court decisions fail or stall and the courts are called upon to make a final judgement on the substance of aboriginal rights? Here there remain some ambiguities.

In *Guerin* v. *R.*,[14] the Musqueam Indian Band had surrendered some land in Vancouver to be leased by the federal government on certain specified terms, with the rental proceeds to be credited to the band. The federal government leased the land on terms that were not as favourable for the band, and the Federal Court of Appeal upheld the federal government's right to do so. The Supreme Court reversed this decision, holding the federal government to fair and honourable dealings and opening up new opportunities for First Nations to raise other historic grievances.

The rhetoric of similarity and difference was used to significantly advance aboriginal rights in this case. In reversing the Federal Court of Appeal's decision, the Supreme Court seemed animated by *similarity:* in any other context — involving non-native players — the need for fair dealing would have been obvious. Beyond this, though, there is reliance on *difference:* unlike non-native landholdings, Musqueam reserve land is held "in trust" by the federal government. This element may yet prove disadvantageous to First Nations in the long run, since it reinforces a hierarchical relationship of dependence. Self-governing peoples do not need other governments to hold land in trust or under "protection" for them.

As we have seen, *the way in which* treaties are interpreted is vital to the interests of aboriginal peoples. The Supreme Court has decided in a string of cases that treaties are to be given a broad and liberal interpretation, consistent with the meaning that aboriginal negotiators would give them. In addition, doubtful expressions are to be decided in favour of First Nations.[15] These cases have usually been concerned with the exercise of some kind of traditional activity, like hunting, and how any guarantees in a treaty would affect provincial legislation intended to restrict such activities. The Supreme Court has interpreted some early treaties very broadly and found such guarantees, which have then prevailed over provincial legislation by virtue of section 88 of the Indian Act. The Act provides that provincial laws of general application apply to Indians, subject to the terms of any treaty.

Such decisions have no doubt advanced aboriginal rights, and the focus on how the First Nations negotiators would have understood the treaty at the time is welcome and appropriate. One limitation of these cases, however, is that they rely on the Indian Act — not the intrinsic nature of treaties — to hold that treaties are paramount over provincial law. Aboriginal rights have been advanced in the name of protecting *federal jurisdiction*, not in recognition of treaties as either a source or an affirmation of aboriginal jurisdiction. Courts have never had doubts (at least until the advent of the Constitution Act 1982), that federal legislation prevailed over treaty rights.[16]

A second weakness in this line of treaty cases (beyond the fact that not all the decisions interpreted the treaties generously) is that the courts have never applied the "as understood by the Indians" test to the sections of the treaty dealing with land cession. It is quite likely that in many cases, contrary to the written text of the treaty, the intent of aboriginal negotiators was not to give up all land rights but to come to an agreement about sharing the land. This conclusion, however, may constitute such a challenge to the legitimacy of the present land tenure system that the courts are hesitant to entertain it seriously.

The newest area of jurisprudence regarding aboriginal rights is the interpretation of section 35 of the Constitution Act 1982, which "recognizes and affirms" existing aboriginal and treaty rights. So far, the Supreme Court has dealt directly with this in only one case, *R. v. Sparrow*.[17] This case dealt with the effect of regulations under the Fisheries Act, which restricted the aboriginal right to fish by regulating the length of net that could be used. Historically, Canadian courts have never doubted that the Fisheries Act took precedence over any treaty or aboriginal rights. Given section 35, however, there were a number of ways the judiciary could approach this question.

One approach favoured by some has been called the "empty box" theory, in which section 35 is understood to be an "empty box" and has no content until further defined by additional constitutional amendments. This view was rationalized by interpreting "existing" rights of aboriginal people as subject to federal legislation prior to 1982, so that the rights guaranteed under section 35 would continue to be subject to federal legislation. In this approach, section 35 alone did not change anything.

The opposite of this theory was the "full box" theory, advanced by the First Nations. In this case, the rights protected in the Constitution were immediately effective and could prevail over federal law.

The "frozen rights" theory offered yet another interpretation: rights protected by section 35 were the rights as they existed in 1982, including whatever restrictions had been placed on them by that date. Given that the word "existing" was added to the constitutional draft at the insistence of a number of provincial premiers over the protests of First Nations, the "frozen rights" theory might actually be fairly close to what the premiers intended.

Faced with this choice of theories in *Sparrow*, the Supreme Court chose none, and set out a more complex theory. "Existing rights," in the Court's view, meant rights that had not been *extinguished* — in this case, an aboriginal right to fish. Before 1982, aboriginal rights could be extinguished, but only if done clearly. *Regulation* of the right to fish, however, was not clear enough to constitute extinguishment of that right. Thus, the regulation of the right prior to 1982 did not affect the right in the abstract: fishing as a right still existed.

Any regulation of an existing aboriginal or treaty right had to pass a test of being "reasonably justified," since the court found that the federal government was responsible for the protection of aboriginal interests, even in exercising its legislative tasks. Among other criteria for being "reasonably justified," the court stipulated that for an aboriginal fishing right to be regulated, the regulation must give priority to the aboriginal fishing rights over all other objectives except conservation. As to whether the regulation at issue was "reasonably justified," the matter was sent back to be examined by the lower courts.

Sparrow, then, represents an ambitious and sensitive attempt to make constitutional room for aboriginal rights. It should be commended for avoiding the pitfalls and sterile reasoning of the "empty box" or "frozen right" theories. The decision's flexibility, and its similarity to the Charter test for the justification of an infringement of a Charter right, will probably guarantee its stability and longevity.

The Court's reasoning, however, may carry liabilities in the long run. The requirement of reasonable justification assumes a hierarchical relationship, in which the federal government is in the paternalistic position of being the protector of aboriginal rights. There is little hint that the rights could exist independently or "inherently." This militates against a frank recognition of aboriginal self-government rights. "Native difference" is the operative frame of reference, and although it is applied here in a way that brings considerable benefit to aboriginal people, it retains the basic hierarchical structure of subjugation.

In this article we have looked at the interplay between "similarity" and "difference" in the way courts have handled aboriginal rights questions. Clearly, it is appropriate that there be such an interplay, since aboriginal people are at once *similar to* and *different from* non-aboriginal people.

The way the courts have historically chosen to invoke similiarity and difference, however, has served to entrench and exacerbate aboriginal disadvantage. Similarity and difference were used to deny First Nations any rights flowing from their status as the original occupants of the land. There was nothing inevitable about how this turned out; it simply represents the political choices made by the courts at that time. Indeed, the case law provides examples of how legal doctrine can be used to the benefit of First Nations. "Similarity" is welcome when it is used to hold the government to fair and honourable dealings with the First Nations. "Difference" is welcome when it is used to make special constitutional room for First Nations. Recent successes in aboriginal rights cases would indicate that using the courts is risky, but potentially beneficial to First Nations.

LEN SAWATSKY

SELF-DETERMINATION AND THE CRIMINAL JUSTICE SYSTEM

THE TREATMENT OF ABORIGINAL people within an adversarial, retributive, European-based criminal justice system graphically demonstrates the need for social and legal change. But how best to accomplish the changes required? Mind-numbing statistics and the horrendous experiences aboriginal people face daily within a system purporting to dispense justice leave advocates of social change settling for expedient measures — those that lie within the realm of the possible. But in order to bring about aboriginal self-determination in criminal justice in a way that is consistent with aboriginal culture, it is essential to determine what method of social change can accomplish this most effectively.

THE NEED FOR A PARADIGM SHIFT

Social change can happen in at least two different ways: gradual improvements to the system — evolution; or starting from scratch with a whole new paradigm — revolution. Most social change efforts in the legal arena seek to reform criminal justice structures through the evolutionary approach, advocating improvements or alternatives where problems in the system can be identified.

Sometimes, however, problems within the system are so pervasive that the system becomes inadequate to handle the situation; at other times, the system itself is the problem. Radical structural change is required. To try to improve such systems by adding on alternatives through the evolutionary process is like patching an old set of clothes with a new unshrunk piece of cloth; it will eventually create an even bigger hole. The evolutionary approach, unfortunately, is proving to be the most insidious form of assimilation ever devised for the native community.

Revolution is a word often associated with violence. But revolutions have taken place in social, cultural and even political arenas without even a hint of direct physical or psychological force. The key to understanding this revolutionary approach to social change is a closer examination of what is meant by a "paradigm" or a "paradigm shift."

When a "scientific revolution" takes place, radical innovation occurs. Scientists look at the subject matter in a *totally different* way. Most scientific advances are simply part of a steady process of innovation and increase of knowledge, but every once in a while, a revolution occurs.[1] For instance, Copernicus theorized that the earth revolved around the sun, rather than the other way around, as was commonly believed. When we realize how much of scientific knowledge, and the resulting inventions that we often take for granted, are hinged upon recognition of such a basic principle as the planets' revolving around the sun, one can begin to appreciate just what a radical shift this really was. The acceptance of the new "paradigm" as a better tool for explaining, predicting, planning and subsequently making applications in associated fields of study is termed a "paradigm shift."

In the social world, differing paradigms exist simultaneously according to the cultural contexts in which they were developed. Institutions, systems and structures that are meant to serve a society are shaped according to the paradigm by which a society defines its reality. The dominant institutions of Canadian society, such as the criminal justice system, view the application of other paradigms, such as aboriginal approaches to criminal justice, as a threat to their existence. Because of their fundamental belief that institutions require one unifying set of rules and principles, these government institutions cannot tolerate other paradigms for justice.

Different approaches to criminal justice do not have to be a threat, however. In seeking alternatives to the way in which the justice system functions for them, First Nations are asserting their desire to determine their own affairs according to their own paradigms for justice. They are not asking to dominate other models. But in order to accommodate their concerns, the dominant institutions will have to be open to a *revolutionary* change of approach.

Policy makers and government officials typically respond to growing public awareness of the inadequacy of the current criminal justice system (and the paradigm which shapes it) by promoting measures that conform to the evolutionary approach to social change. Such measures include affirmative action efforts, court communicator programs, RCMP Special Constables, Youth Justice Committees and a variety of outreach programs sponsored by various parts of the criminal justice system. This is not to discourage the development of such programs, but simply to identify them as efforts to fix or patch up the system *as it is*. These measures do not bring about fundamental and structural change in the system itself, and they certainly do not serve the purposes of aboriginal self-determination except in a liberal, individualistic sense.

That government institutions may at times be open to *evolutionary* change should not be surprising, even in the criminal justice system. When faced with the need for change, the evolutionary approach does not seriously challenge the institution itself or those who work within it. In fact, it enhances its power. Gradually improving the system, ensuring that a percentage of the total workforce within a department reflects the proportion of aboriginal people within the country or the province, simply legitimizes that structure.

Such ironies continue, however. Most people recognize that the Indian Act of Canada effectively thwarts aboriginal governance and that the Department of Indian Affairs derives its reason for being from the Indian Act, which virtually all aboriginal groups would like to see thrown out once and for all. And yet the department tries to make sure that its workforce reflects the percentage of aboriginal people in the country. The same is true in the criminal justice system, which is based on a "retributive" paradigm for justice. While the bureaucrats are trying to get more aboriginal guards for this country's prisons, they ignore the fact that punishment, guilt and cages for humans have no precedents in aboriginal cultural traditions.

The evolutionary approach clearly serves the purposes of assimilation, not self-determination. It may not be as obvious and coercive a tactic as what we now understand the residential schools to have been, but the "gradual improvement" approach can be used to serve the same purposes. Some have conjectured that the residential schools of yesterday have become the prisons of today. What can be more dismaying than soliciting aboriginal individuals to be guards in these prisons?

ABORIGINAL VIEWS OF JUSTICE[2]

"Culturally consistent" self-determination in the criminal justice area necessitates a revolutionary approach to change. This is so for a number of reasons.

Aboriginal ways of doing justice are based on an entirely different paradigm than that of the Canadian criminal justice system. Native culture is shaped by distinct ways of viewing time and physical reality. Unlike European-based world views, aboriginal people see time as circular, not linear, and acknowledge a oneness of humanity with the created order. In order to implement their unique customs, laws, traditions and ways of life, aboriginal people require autonomy and formal recognition as legitimate nation builders.

For aboriginal people, norms and laws are inherent in the natural order, not imposed from the outside. The "state" is a foreign concept; justice depends upon the internal order and relations of a given society or community. All of this suggests a very different response to individuals who do not conform to social expectations in aboriginal societies. When deviations from the norm and conflicting interests break the harmony of aboriginal communities, the traditional way of responding is to do whatever is necessary to restore harmony. Long before white people settled in this country, a peacemaker role was a vital component in aboriginal communities.

To give you a better understanding of the paradigms identified above, the following table compares the distinct characteristics of each.[3]

European and Aboriginal Paradigms for Criminal Justice

European/Retributive	Aboriginal
1. Crime defined as violation of the state	No word for crime but recognition of injury, harm, conflicts and disputes
2. Focus on establishing blame, guilt, on the past (did he/she do it?)	Focus on identifying the conflict, on establishing accountability, on the current situation (what can we do?)
3. Adversarial relationships and process are normative	Consensus of elders/chiefs to advise on steps to take towards establishing harmony
4. Imposition of pain to punish and deter/prevent	Holding parties in conflict accountable to each other in context of family, community and Mother Earth.
5. Justice defined by intent and by process, right rules	Justice defined by social harmony and needs being met, judged according to community solidarity and survival
6. Interpersonal, conflictual nature of crime obscured, repressed: conflict seen as individual vs. state	Interpersonal conflict acknowledged in the context of responsibility to family, community and Mother Earth
7. One social injury replaced by another	Focus on repair of social injury and restoration of social equilibrium and healing

8. Community on sideline, represented abstractly by state

Community as facilitator, role of the elder respected

9. Encouragement of competitive individualistic values

Encouragement of spirituality, self-esteem and collective identity

10. Action directed from state to offender:
 — victim ignored
 — offender passive

Recognition of victim's needs and offender accountability but in the context of wisdom and insight exercised by elders

11. Offender accountability defined as taking punishment

Offender accountability defined as willingness to take steps to restore peace and harmony with self, victim, families, community and the Great Spirit

12. Offence defined in purely legal terms, devoid of moral, social, economic or political dimensions

Offence understood in whole context — morally, socially, economically, politically and in relation to the land

13. "Debt" owed to state and society in abstract

Offender is held accountable to the victim, victim's family and community

14. No encouragement or opportunity to express remorse or forgiveness

Encouragement for apology, forgiveness and healing with a view to making peace

15. Dependence upon proxy professionals

Direct involvement of participants to the dispute under guidance of elders

Cultural distinctions are not the only factors that suggest a different way of doing justice. Aboriginal peoples do not perceive the adversarial, retributive model of criminal justice as being an adequate response to the problem of crime. For one thing, it does not meet the need of either the victim or the offender. From an aboriginal perspective, victims need to meet the offender face to face, receive personal restitution and be directly involved in a fair settlement.[4] Likewise, offenders must meet the victim face to face and understand the actual consequences of their actions. They must be held accountable and take direct responsiblility for repairing the damage and restoring harmonious relations in the community. The experience of punishment and imprisonment damages the human spirit and usually encourages further harmful behaviour.[5]

Aboriginal self-determination in the criminal justice area is further warranted as a response to the appalling over-representation of aboriginal people entangled in the criminal justice system. There is much to suggest that the criminal justice system is systemically racist. In 1989, aboriginal people represented approximately 6 percent of the general population of Manitoba and 54 percent of the provincial jail population.[6] Disproportionate incarceration rates for aboriginal people exist in every province and territory of Canada, but the very worst exist in the Yukon and Northwest Territories, Saskatchewan and Manitoba.

The reasons for this are complex, but the following research findings give some indication of why aboriginal people show up in prisons in disproportionate numbers:

1. Because of deferential surveillance and intervention policies, aboriginal people are more likely to be arrested and charged with an offence.[7]
2. Because of economic deprivation, aboriginal people are forced to rely on Legal Aid lawyers with high caseloads; research shows that this generally results in a higher rate of guilty pleas and/or findings.[8]
3. Despite the offsetting influence of fine option programs, aboriginal people are still falling through the cracks. Natives are most frequently charged with minor provincial and municipal offenses for which the usual disposition is a fine. Because of their high unemployment rates, they are less likely to be able to pay the fine and eventually end up in jail.
4. Aboriginal offenders are more likely than non-native offenders to be incarcerated for a violent offence.[9]
5. Aboriginal inmates are less likely to get full parole than non-natives and more likely to be returned to prison for technical violations of their parole.[10]

Aboriginal justice programs based on cultural traditions overlap with some of the programs arising out of the "mediation" movement in Canada. But while victim-offender mediation and reconciliation or community work service programs are better than incarceration, non-native mediation programs often function as add-ons or play a supplementary role to the mainstream criminal justice system. To avoid assimilation or absorption into the retributive-adversarial justice system of mainstream society, and to assert aboriginal self-determination instead, aboriginal justice projects should strive to be integral, indigenous and relatively independent.

ONE SOLUTION

The Native Harmony and Restoration Centre (NHRC) has been set up at the Interlake Reserves Tribal Council in Manitoba to establish a corrections-based program that conforms to the aboriginal justice paradigm. It aims to be a comprehensive, integrated demonstration of the traditional Ojibway peacemaker role. Through the use of mediation, restitution, reparation, community work service, reconciliation and traditional healing, the NHRC is seeking to provide services as an expression of self-determination and cultural consistency.

The mission statement of the NHRC states that the Centre "shall provide a comprehensive rehabilitational environment for offenders and services for victims based on culturally consistent aboriginal justice traditions." The goals of the NHRC are:

1. to provide a physical, social, educational, vocational and therapeutic setting in which rehabilitation can take place according to values of aboriginal cultures.
2. to restore aboriginal persons in conflict with the law into harmony with themselves, the victims of their actions, their families and communities.
3. to instil a sense of worth, dignity and accountability within aboriginal offenders in the context of native cultures and values.
4. to eliminate the over-incarceration of aboriginal people.

The program objectives include:

1. resolving conflicts between disputants through the use of mediation, counselling, conflict resolution, community service work or any other reasonable settlements;
2. establishing and nurturing a healthy family life for offenders and giving them the ability to function effectively as members of a group or community;
3. promoting self-awareness and self-esteem in offenders by encouraging a strong aboriginal identity and spirituality;
4. facilitating the development of the attitudes and skills required for residents to become active and productive participants in community living;
5. providing opportunities for work and service that attempt to redress the harm and injury inflicted upon a victim (individual or community) by an offender;
6. providing residents with opportunities for education, vocational training and employment experience that will generate realistic career opportunities once they leave the Centre;
7. offering the recreational, social service and mental and physical health resources required to address specific and identifiable personal and social problems;
8. working in close co-operation with Reserve communities in order to bring about successful reintegration of Centre residents when they return to their respective communities.[11]

Aboriginal self-government is not an empty container that needs to be filled with European or American notions and practices. Even within the restrictions of economic deprivation, it is essential to assume that aboriginal culture is a full container that has within it all that is required to maintain law and order, prevent crime, apply sanctions, restore positive social relations and repair them. The major limitation preventing aboriginal peoples from moving towards full expression lies, of course, in their history of economic marginalization and dependence, and the failure of successive federal and provincial governments to honour the treaties made by representatives of the Crown.

Naturally, such a history does undermine and erode the culture of a people. But recent events in Canada, such as the defeat of the Meech Lake Accord, the conflict at Oka and aboriginal participation in the 1992 constitutional negotiations have amply demonstrated that aboriginal traditions are alive and well. With the dismal failure of the criminal justice system in North America and the noncredibility of the retributive paradigm that guides it, First Nations may well provide some desperately needed leadership. Rather than viewing aboriginal governance as a threat, Canadians might look to the application of an aboriginal justice paradigm to bring about the safe, secure and harmonious communities we all desire.

II

COMMUNITIES IN TRANSITION

M A G G I E   H O D G S O N

REBUILDING COMMUNITY AFTER THE RESIDENTIAL SCHOOL EXPERIENCE

Stories have a way of speaking to the mind, spirit and emotions; they become a metaphor for life. Two aboriginal stories, one from the Maoris in Aukland, New Zealand, and one from the United States, speak to me about perception, and about vision, pain and hope.

The first story, from New Zealand, is about a shark who was swimming through an ocean he had discovered. The shark met a mackerel. And just before he swallowed the mackerel for dinner, the shark offered a suggestion. "Let's assimilate!" he said.

Now, from whose perspective do we look at this story? The shark thinks he is doing the mackerel a favour because he will provide him with a nice warm stomach to swim around in. The mackerel's perception is different. He thinks, "If it is at all possible, I do not want to end up as part of that shark. I am a mackerel and free . . . and I intend to remain free."

The second story is about a number of Hopi elders in the mid-1850s. During a ceremony they were given a prophecy:

"Our people are in our midnight and we will come into our daylight when the eagle lands on the moon. When the eagle lands on the moon we will become world leaders." The old people did not know what that prophecy meant, but they trusted it and handed it down from generation to generation. In 1969, when American astronauts first landed on the moon, the message they sent back to earth was: "The Eagle has landed!" When our elders heard this news via satellite, they finally knew what the prophecy meant.

They knew that our "midnight" represented the breach of the treaties, the outlawing of traditional Indian ceremonies, the establishment of the residential school system, the presence of violence, alcoholism and pain. Our people knew the time had come for change! At that point, our society began a transformation. We started to become the leaders of social and environmental healing. We were finally moving "into our daylight."

Before the day dawned, however, most Canadian history and most government policies were written from the point of view of the shark in the first story. The resulting breakdown of tradition and of family structures led to self-destruction in the form of violence and alcoholism.

OUTLAWING CEREMONY

"Let's assimilate" . . . In the late 1800s and early 1900s, the Canadian government declared illegal the practice of native ceremonies, such as the Potlatch and the Sundance. Taking away these and other ceremonies meant taking away the ideas, values and principles basic to community mental health. With the ceremonies went security, ideology, rituals, belonging, beliefs, access to resources, time together, healing and justice. The destruction of ceremonies was the core of the Canadian government's genocidal policies and it served as a knife cutting out the heart of the culture.

"Let's assimilate" . . . The government also replaced the system of traditional chiefs with a system of elected chiefs. With this move, they removed a process for consensus, role modelling

and management based on the value of relationships. They replaced it with a competitive hierarchical system of management-by-objectives. The new system focused the communities on only a piece of the picture, blurring the picture as a whole, and often dividing communities.

RESIDENTIAL SCHOOLS AND FAMILY BREAKDOWN

"Let's assimilate" . . . One of the most insidious tools of assimilation was the residential school system. Set up and run primarily by churches on behalf of the federal government, the residential schools, in effect, formalized family breakdown as a matter of national policy. They delivered a further blow to First Nations cultures and had a profound impact on native mental health.

Most of the first missionaries were very hardy and committed to living with and amongst native peoples. They learned the language; they learned how to survive the harshness of the climate. They taught native people farming and writing. The First Nations reciprocated, teaching the missionaries survival in the harsh climate. The arrangement was based on mutuality.

The large formalized residential schools attracted a new breed of missionaries. Some really cared about the young people they were in charge of, but had been trained in a system that taught harshness and therefore they treated their students harshly. They were taught to believe that the more they sacrificed and denied their humanity, the closer they would be to God. Their seminaries and postulants' houses were not houses of warmth and love but places of sacrifice to God; places where you denied human comforts as a sign of commitment. They expected their students to hold the same values.

Many of the nuns and priests had left home in their formative years. The loneliness of being away from their culture and families may have affected their lives deeply. In their religious education, they were taught to fear God's damnation for not saving the souls of "superstitious" children who believed that the land, rocks and plants had spirits. They also learned to cover up their own pain and offer it to God. They learned a form of discipline that was punitive and shaming. Some older nuns talk about having to whip themselves for the sins they committed — like thinking that the Mother Superior was an "old witch" — when training to become a nun. The system was based on "sin" and "good" and "bad," a radically different ideology than the one native children had learned at home. By watching role models, like grandparents, the children were taught that you learn from your mistakes.

The children were transported to residential school by wagon, boat, car and, later, plane, under the authority of the Indian agent, the RCMP and the priests. It was impossible to challenge such authority, which represented the government, the police and the Church. Parents would be threatened with a jail sentence if they did not co-operate — either that or the Indian agent would cut off the family's rations.

To give you a better idea of what it was like for the children to be carted off to residential schools, imagine what it would be like if all the white Canadian five-year-old children were moved to Japan, under Japanese guard, and they all had to live there until they were fifteen to twenty years old. Imagine also that they had to speak Japanese, learn Buddhism, participate in all Japanese customs, and never speak in their mother tongue. They would not be allowed to participate in any Canadian practice or ceremony during their years in Japan.

Imagine that your children had to be pulled from your arms and taken to Japan, not to be seen for months, years or perhaps ever. Imagine that all your children were taken. Would you not feel an agonizing feeling of failure that you could not even protect your children? Would you not feel a loss of hope? Would you not feel a deep, deep loneliness? Would you not fear for their safety? Would you not worry about who would teach them the family rituals, especially if your whole social system was built on the family and ceremonies? How would you cope?

What if three successive generations were moved to Japan in this way? What would be left of the values of your culture and language or of the meaning of your whole social system?

What would you do if you were a child being removed from your parents' arms? Would you scream, "Mom, help! Mom, help!"? What would you do if you saw your parents standing there helplessly? Would you feel, "They should have stopped them from taking me"? What would you feel if you arrived in that big building where there were people speaking a funny language and when you spoke the language you knew, you were hit and told to speak in that strange language? What if your culture taught that your hair was part of your spirit, and the strange people cut off all your hair and scrubbed your head with something that burned your scalp to get rid of "lice"? What if you were bathed in a public washroom? What would you do with the shame? What would you do if you saw your brother or sister and you ran to them and were hit for speaking to them?

How much fear and loneliness would you feel? Probably the same amount as those children did. In residential school, grieving over loss of contact with parents often had to happen under your blankets or in your pillow — it would be repressed in order not to give the people who took you away the benefit of seeing your pain. It's natural for children to cry when they are hurt, scared or need attention. If in your home of origin you experienced parental response to your crying, you would expect to receive a response now. What if the only response you got for crying was being hit? Maybe the occasional nun or priest would pay attention to you. But whom would you trust? Whom could you trust?

INCONGRUENCE AND ABUSE: THE SHARK'S SUCCESS?

In experiences like these we find the foundation of loneliness and hopelessness, alcoholism and suicide. We have to be able — to be willing — to trust, to talk about our pain and to show pain.

Fear is a significant factor in mental breakdown, suicide, sexual abuse and violence. Fear and loneliness are the two deepest emotions alcoholics experience and those two emotions impede their ability to reach out. Not having power or control over our lives increases fear and the sense of powerlessness. The need for power and control is a key factor motivating violence.

My mother was at the Lejac Residential School in B.C. from 1911 to 1922. She was not allowed to go home for the first five years because the school was too far away. Her mother had died in childbirth, and when her father remarried during her time at school, my mother lost track of him. Some of the children died in the 1918 flu epidemic and their parents never saw them again. Other children lost track of their families, since they often moved with the migrating animals for hunting and trapping purposes and there were no mail systems. Often the parents could not write English and so were unable to send a letter by any means. Parents were also restrained by law from leaving their reserves and so could not move closer to their children's school.

The children learned to read and write, they learned to speak English and they learned to farm. They also learned that the "special" roles of priest and nun meant special food that the children could not have. This even happened when I went to school: the nuns had butter and we had margarine. They had fresh fruit and we didn't. Those children learned what I did — how to steal from the sisters' cooler and how to lie when you were caught. It taught them how to say "yes" when they sometimes felt like telling the nun to take a flying leap off a deep cliff to where Lucifer resides. It taught some to hate and feel hopeless.

Incongruence is a survival behaviour. It creates confusion, pain and loneliness because we have a desire to be seen and loved as we are, not as the image we feel we have to project to be safe. It creates dissociation from pain, which is the foundation of survival for a child who is in an unsafe position and cannot cope with the pain anymore. It is also a symptom of people who drink in an attempt to escape from their emotional pain, and of people who are mentally unstable.

I went to Catholic boarding school at my mother's insistence because she was a practising alcoholic and she thought I would be "safe" there. Thus, I became a victim of residential school through the second generation. My response to boarding school was to become angry and resistant. For thirty-two years I was unable to express my anger with my mother for sending me to boarding school, because I was taught to "honour your father and mother." So I turned my anger inward, even attempting suicide. Later I turned my anger towards all the injustice I saw in society. My fears, loneliness and feelings of abandonment were no different than my mother's. The difference was that in 1959 I could "lip off" in anger to the nuns.

The residential schools eliminated familiar social rituals that helped establish a sense of security and safety. The schools eliminated time spent with the extended family and changed ideology and beliefs. By cutting children off from their communities the schools effectively cut off access to traditional teachings about living on the land and having respect for all creatures. But children found ways to recreate family among their peers. The friendships and bonding that evolved from their five to ten years together away from their families set into motion lifetime friendships for many of them. They also learned to seek out the gentle nuns and nurturing priests. They set up surrogate families.

Some of the people employed in the residential schools as "dorm supervisors" were not missionaries and some were physically, verbally and sexually abusisve. One such man, who worked at St. George's Indian Residential School in Lytton, British Columbia, abused at least 140 boys.[1]

Two of his victims testified at a court hearing that he had committed over six hundred acts of buggery. They didn't know it was happening to the other children too. They were filled with shame and guilt, because they blamed themselves for what happened. Imagine that repressed shame! Often the kids who ran away were brought back by the Mounties and then beaten by the priests.

Imagine if you told someone you trusted — say, one of the "good" nuns — that someone had abused you, and she told you to "pray for him." She probably said that because she believed that it would help you, and because she feared the exposure if what happened to you might be known to the general community. Her attitude about sexual abuse and how to deal with it would not be much different than the prevalent attitude about sexual abuse in Canadian society at that time. If you didn't know what to do about sexual abuse, you didn't talk about it. Some of the brothers, priests and nuns were themselves sexual abusers.

Perhaps the most pervasive form of abuse was the verbal violence from nuns and priests. The children were called "dirty Indians," "savages." My mom was called a "bastard" because she didn't have a family to go to until her aunt and uncle started to take her during the holidays.

There was also physical violence, a practice stemming from the accepted belief in mainstream society that if you "spare the rod" you "spoil the child." To children who had come from a society where discipline meant you learned from your own mistakes and from your grandparents and other role models, the rod spelled only fear and alienation.

The violence affected not only individual children, but also whole families and future generations. In one community where I conducted a sexual abuse workshop, a woman came in with big scars all over her face. Her nose had nearly been cut off — the knife-cut still showed, no more than half an inch from the tip of her nose. Her husband, who had beaten her, was a convicted sexual abuser; he had also been a victim of abuse in residential school. In the workshop, participants, including members of the husband's family, told about some of the sexual abuse they had suffered when they were young. His brother was the only one in the family who had not been abused, and he wondered how he had managed to escape.

The violent brother, the man who had cut up his wife, told the non-abused brother a story from residential school. "Remember how I used to get you up every night to go pee?" he asked. His brother remembered. "The reason I did that was because when I wet the bed, the priest would take me to his room and rape me and then he would beat me for wetting the bed. I never wanted that to happen to you, so I used to get you up to pee."

The brother he had saved from abuse had gone on to be a successful athlete, had travelled to Europe with his team, had an education, was a non-drinker and a leader. But the man who had heroically protected his brother as a boy was now a violent practising alcoholic, who was locked in pain and abused his wife with knives and fists.

If you subject one generation of children to physical and verbal abuse and they become adults and have children, and then you subject that generation and a third generation to a residential school system, you have a whole society affected by isolation, loneliness, sadness, anger, hopelessness and pain.

In his book *Le suicide*, French sociologist Emile Durkheim writes that when you reach into a culture and pull out the values, rituals and societal norms and you attempt to inject new values, rituals and societal norms, you risk creating a society that suffers from *anomie* — disorientation and absence of values. Those of our people who have difficulty adjusting, who are in jail, who are alcoholics, who suffer from poor self-esteem, are actually reflecting the effects of the Canadian government's residential school policies and the misguided involvement of the Church in carrying out some of those policies. They reflect Canadian laws that restricted native religious practices, changed our traditional leadership, limited travel off the reserves, and forced native children to attend residential schools.

"THE EAGLE HAS LANDED": HEALING AND HOPE

The Hopi prophecy said that "our people will come out of our midnight and come into our daylight when the eagle lands on the moon." Broken treaties, disrupted family life, alcoholism, high rates of incarceration — all these have been seen as "our midnight."

But within the past few years we have embraced the truth of that prophecy. The grief and pain of several generations is finally turning into healthy reflection and healing. The courage, grit and determination of some of our elders led them to hide the ceremonies and continue them in secret. Their foresight during the time the children were away at residential school helped families to come back together and rebuild a new version of Indian culture. One step at a time, we are developing mutual respect between native and non-native people for a new kind of societal development.

Aboriginal communities started to deal with alcoholism in 1969 — the year the astronauts sent the message from the moon that "the Eagle has landed." From the beginning, programs were set up on the premise of building a vision of sobriety and reintroducing ritual and its meaning, ceremony, healing and community. The vision of committed individuals became the vision of whole communities. Alkali Lake, British Columbia, went from 100 percent alcoholism in the early seventies, to 95 percent sobriety today. Cold Lake, Alberta, moved from 25 percent sobriety in 1984 to 65 percent by 1988. It's now possible to have five thousand people turn out to a sober pow-wow in Edmonton.

The process of change has resulted in more community development, training programs for health workers to inform the public about addiction treatment, treatment programs and after-care and the reintroduction and reinforcement of a sense of community. The Nechi Institute in Edmonton, Alberta, trains addiction counsellors from within a native model of spirituality and assists communities seeking to reclaim a lifestyle of health and wholeness. Recently, on O'Chiese Reserve, virtually the whole community — children, youth, parents, grandparents and elders — spent several weeks in a unique community-based program. It included information on addiction, co-dependency and family violence, and personal stories of healing. Recreational and artistic activities and spiritual ceremonies also helped to promote an addiction-free way of life in the community. As belief and ideology are rebuilt, as resources are made available within our communities and as community justice is re-established, feelings of safety are again possible. Instead of living in fear we can live and work with hope and action.

Alcohol treatment programs address a multitude of problems. In some communities, all candidates for office in band councils must be abstainers, because they are considered to be role models. Imagine if such rules existed in the mainstream — what a vision!

In Alberta a new commitment to mental health is reflected

in the fact that 1600 native people are seeing therapists. We do not have statistics on the number of people who see elders for healing because our old people have not hooked up to computers yet, relying strictly on the relationship they have with the Creator and their success in treating our people for spiritual as well as emotional and physical health.

Partnerships are being built with government and non-native agencies, based on the understanding that we have something to learn from each other. In this new system, neither is the "shark" nor the "mackerel"; we are part of one school of fish working to make the world a healthier place. In Alberta, we are currently using provincial mental health workers as co-trainers of native addiction workers at the Nechi Institute. The province donates staff to work with us, and we donate our staff to provide cross-cultural experience. Non-native mental health workers are often not successful at maintaining the relationship with their native clients. By working as co-trainers, however, they are able to learn more effective approaches to working with our people. In turn, we learn more about clinical approaches to restoring mental health.

There are over 350 native alcohol treatment and prevention programs across Canada, which are managed by native people and funded by Health and Welfare Canada. The National Native Alcohol and Drug Abuse Program, organized by native leaders working in the addictions field, receives most of its funding from Health and Welfare Canada. Through its annual "National Addictions Awareness Week" campaign, the program has widely increased awareness of alcoholism as a Canadian social problem that is not limited to native communities. Participation has increased dramatically. In 1987, twenty-five native communities were involved; only five years later, in 1992, 1657 native and non-native communities across Canada were participating in substance abuse prevention campaigns and celebrating success. No provincial or federal health promotion campaign can claim that kind of increase — 6600 percent — in voluntary community participation.

A vision of restored health goes beyond Canadian borders. A conference with the theme "Healing Our Spirit Worldwide" was held in Edmonton in July 1992. Initiated by the Nechi Institute and its sister organization, Poundmaker Lodge, the conference brought together 3500 people from all over the world to look at all aspects of healing in aboriginal communities.

The prophecy of the 1850s is coming true. Our people are allowing that vision of healing and leadership to shape the ways they deal with the issues facing them. Yes, the eagle has landed!

BURTON JACOBS

THE INDIAN AGENT SYSTEM AND OUR MOVE TO SELF-GOVERNMENT

A STORY IS TOLD about an Indian agent who struck up a conversation with a stranger. The stranger asked the agent what sort of work he did, and the agent said: "I'm an Indian agent." The stranger replied: "That's interesting. What kind of products do you sell?" The agent said: "I sell Indians."

There was a time, not too long ago, when Indian agents flourished on Indian reserves. During their heyday, all business and all personal contacts to a reserve had to be made through them. This peculiar situation was the result of the way land title was set up.

All land title on a reserve is vested in Her Majesty's name, and the Indian agent, being an agent of the Crown, was the only person authorized to sign contracts that were in any way associated with the reserve. And since all business directly or

This article is excerpted from an address by Burton Jacobs to the Society for Applied Anthropology Annual Meeting, March 16, 1984. First published in *Walpole Island: The Struggle for Self Sufficiency — A Panel Presentation,* Occasional Paper no. 3, edited by Sheila M. Van Wyck. Nin.da.waab.jig, Walpole Island, May 1984.

indirectly dealt with reserve land, this meant that the agent had his hand in practically everything. The agent was the top dog, and there was no mistaking it.

By virtue of the Indian Act, all administrative matters relating to an Indian reserve were under the direct control of the Indian agent. The chief and council were virtually powerless because the agent had systematic control of the council. He attended every council meeting, and he insisted that no council meeting was official unless he was present. He generally came into the council meeting with a list of items that he wanted the council to pass, and the council generally passed them without question or without any argument. And if a councillor expressed a point of view that was unpopular with the agent, he would intrude and argue the point. He generally ended the argument by saying that he "would not recommend it." Invariably, the resolutions were approved or rejected in Ottawa according to the agent's recommendations.

Under these conditions any race of people would find it very difficult to achieve any measure of success in their living. History has proven that; in all the years that the agents had been acting for the Indian people, they made no significant advancements.

Knowing this to be true, and after living under an autocratic rule that left us with no hope for a better future, I, with the support of others, began to think it was time for a change. I began to develop this thought further when I became chief in 1960, although at that time I had no clear idea what approach I should take. But after I had a series of big disagreements with the agent, I knew what I had to do. I would have to do my darnedest to kick him out.

I decided to go from door to door with a petition to try to solicit support for my cause. This was a very slow and difficult process. I had no problem with those people who had frequent contacts with the agent because they knew what it was like to deal with him. I had problems with older people and with those who did not have frequent contacts with the agent. They were afraid of change. They thought that if a new system was introduced, perhaps we would lose more. Even though this was a very slow and difficult process, there was never a time when I thought I should quit.

One day, after I had been at work for about a year soliciting support, I was surprised to see the Indian agent at my door.

He said: "I understand that you are trying to get rid of me."

I said that was true.

"Perhaps we should talk about this," he said.

So, I took him under the shade of a thorn tree by the river and we sat down on a bench. He talked and talked and said that what I was doing was wrong, and that I was creating a disturbance and stirring up the people. He said that if I continued to create unrest in the community, it would be difficult to get any work done. He pleaded that I should have a heart and be more compassionate. I did not say anything.

When he finished talking, I told him I would think it over. The agent left, and I thought to myself that this was going to be the beginning of a long, drawn-out battle. I knew he was going to put up a lot of resistance and that he was going to use every means to get me out of office.

The next episode may be coincidental, but I began to receive a lot of attention from the police. They stopped my car a number of times and did a thorough search. They looked into the glove compartment, inside the car and in the trunk. They didn't say what they were looking for, and I didn't ask them, but I suspected that they were trying to force me to stop what I was doing.

The next move the agent took was to exercise his authority as a truant officer. He took me to court on a charge that I had kept my daughter out of school without a valid cause. Fortunately, I obtained my daughter's medical record from her doctor and presented this to the judge, who dismissed the case.

It appeared now that the agent was intensifying his campaign. He used any excuse to attack me and any councillors he thought were my supporters. This had the effect of stirring up a hornet's nest. One councillor was very annoyed, and he made a lot of noise about this when his boy was sent to reform school.

I took advantage of this hostile climate to solidify my position, thinking this was an opportune time to enlist support from those councillors who were undecided or uncommitted.

We began to have a series of private meetings, or secret

meetings, in homes, changing our location each time. We planned to hold our last big meeting in an old, abandoned school on the main road. We decided beforehand that no cars should be parked around the school so we would not arouse any suspicion.

When the next council meeting took place, I went to the council hall earlier than usual. I wanted very much to have this eviction matter dealt with as soon as possible, while the councillors were in the right frame of mind. Human nature being what it is, they could very easily lose their momentum if discussions were drawn out too long.

I was glad to see councillor Simpson Brigham arrive at the council hall. He was in good spirits, and did not seem to be nervous at all. He introduced his eviction motion to the council, and it was voted upon and carried with a clear majority. The motion was like a bomb that exploded on the floor, knocking the wind out of those who were struck by it. The agent and two councillors never said one word during the entire meeting.

This was only one of many battles that had to be fought. Even before the smoke cleared, another enemy appeared on the scene in the form of a Citizens' Committee organized for the express purpose of fighting the council. They invaded our council meeting in a large force and sat there whispering, giggling, and sometimes interjecting during the course of the council proceedings. Their purpose was to block motions by intimidation and to collect any evidence they could use to get us out of office.

The committee was composed of Indian people who were close to the Indian agent and three employees of the council. They were present at every council meeting, and although they did not create any great problem, the real danger was the possibility that they could grow in numbers.

Once, after a council meeting, one or two of the group came up to me and told me I should call a public meeting to explain why the council dismissed the Indian agent. I told them I would be glad to do that and I would post notices to inform the public. I told my councillors that the Citizens' Committee wanted a public meeting and to be sure to be there because it would be very important.

When the time came to have the public meeting, I didn't see one councillor in the crowd — not even one! They had all forgotten to come.

But the Citizens' Committee hadn't forgotten. They were all there with all their members. There were also a lot of other people there who didn't forget to come. The absence of the councillors, I am sure, was a blessing in disguise, since it reduced the number of targets. There was also another advantage; it gave my talk continuity.

I didn't wait for the councillors to arrive; I got right down to business. I started off by saying: "I suppose you people want to know why we want to get rid of the agent. The answer is very simple. I'm tired of being kicked around by the agents, and I'm sure there are a lot of people here who are also sick and tired. If you people think the agents have done some good for us, I would like to know what they have done. The agents have been around one hundred years, and during that time we haven't moved a foot forward. In fact, I think we have moved backwards. If you don't believe me, just step outside the reserve a little ways and see the big difference between their community and ours. No one can tell me that the Indian agents have done any good for us."

After my little talk, I gave the Citizens' Committee the opportunity to say whatever they wanted to say. Surprisingly, no one wanted to say anything. There was only one who said that we shouldn't allow outside persons to come in and take our jobs away. That was precisely my point in getting rid of the agent. We wanted to start to do things for ourselves.

When I couldn't get any more responses, I adjourned the meeting. Afterwards, a lot of the people came forward to shake my hand and pat me on the back. They said I had done a wonderful job and wondered how I could have managed it. I felt very good.

The Citizens' Committee's unsuccessful attempt to win public support did not stop them in their work. They still attended every council meeting, presumably hoping they would break up the council in some way.

One evening, before the start of a council meeting, we noticed that there were no Citizens' Committee members around. We wondered what had happened. Then an informer, who had just arrived at the council hall, told us that the committee was on its way to Ottawa to petition the minister to remove the chief and councillors from office because of their subversive activity.

We went into a huddle and had a very quick meeting. We decided to follow the Citizens' Committee to Ottawa and present our side of the story to the minister. At the close of the council meeting, I asked the agent to make an appointment for the council to see the minister. The following morning I asked the agent whether he had made the appointment. He said that he had forgotten. Knowing that we could not depend on the agent, we boarded a train in Chatham and left for Ottawa.

In Ottawa we met with a departmental director. We told him what we wanted — we wanted the agent removed. But the director started to talk; he said that the agent was a good fellow and had done a lot of good; he had heard a lot of good reports about this agent. I said that maybe from the agent's point of view everything was okay, but from where we sat, the conditions were terrible. We still said we wanted the agent removed.

But the director was still stubborn. Then one of the councillors, Simpson Brigham, spoke up, and said: "If you can't grant us our request, we're going to resign and call a press conference."

The director got a little nervous and said, "You can't do that. We'll adjourn this meeting and continue the dialogue later on."

During the next nine months, the rivalry between the council, the agent and the Citizens' Committee went on as usual. There didn't seem to be any let-up.

Round about this time, the Citizens' Committee demanded that our books be audited. They said that we were misappropriating funds, that we were creating a disturbance and that conditions on the reserve were terrible. An auditor came around and spent two days looking over our books.

I was a little nervous about this because even if a slight discrepancy was found, they could use that as an excuse to deny us our request for self-government. But fortunately everything proved to be all right. Our books were in good order, and the conditions on the reserve did not warrant our removal.

The next move the council made was to dismiss three employees who were members of the Citizens' Committee. I don't like to consider this a retaliatory move; I like to think of it as a reorganizational move. When the motion was introduced, however, the mover got kind of carried away. The motion called for the dismissal of all council employees with the exception of a secretary.

This decision seems to have stimulated some activity on the part of the department because the next day I had a call from the Toronto District Office saying: "Bring your council down to my office for a two-day meeting; we'll try to grant you your self-government on a trial basis for one year."

Well, we had a two-day meeting there and with some difficulty, we came up with some terms that were satisfactory to both parties.

After about a year, Indian Affairs made an assessment of our operation and they were very satisfied. They said self-government was a success, and they started to promote this all across Canada. We had visitors from every province in the Dominion. The seven chiefs from the Maritime provinces presented me with a traditional talking stick. (This is a stick used in traditional council gatherings. The stick is passed from person to person, and one is allowed to address the council only when holding the stick.)

In the space of five years after we went under self-government, we started and completed development programs that cost well in excess of $2.75 million. We built a bridge that cost over $1 million. We built a large school that cost over $1 million. And we built the first day care on an Indian reserve in Canada. That's something we are proud of.

NAPES ASHINI

NITASSINAN: CARIBOU AND F-16S

It was the month of August. I believe it was 1939. We started to move inland to hunt, fish, trap; to live as a family. Your mother, Mary Agatha, was the youngest. She was three years old, Sebastian was a year older and Madeleine was the oldest. We only took about one hundred pounds of flour, some sugar, baking powder, salt, matches, tea and ammunition, and our canoe.

So we go up the river, Uashau Shipu, on our way to Mishikamau Nipi, some five hundred miles to the northwest. The portages and lakes we used were a major route used by Innu going inland with their families. Several families travelled with us in canoes.

It was an arduous journey . . . there is a portage called Uinipeku Paushtuk that is more than thirty miles long. After portaging our canoe on my back, I had to go back for all the rest of our gear. And of course your grandmother and the children had to walk. This happens every day.

This article has also appeared in *Alternatives Journal* vol. 18 no. 2 (University of Waterloo) and *Perception* vols 15-4/16-1 (Canadian Council on Social Development). The passages in italic type are the words of the author's grandfather, Pien Selma, as he told his story to Napes. The passages in roman type represent the author's own words and ideas from 1991. Together they form the historical and contemporary picture.

Your grandmother Enen, she works hard too; patching our tent, gathering firewood, caring for the children. When we men went hunting together and made a kill, the meat was shared. Eventually the time came for the families to go their different directions, hoping to meet again in spring. By then it was the last week in October and getting colder.

Archaeologists have evidence of our people having been here for nine thousand years. None of this land, our land has ever been ceded to any other government. We have never signed any treaties. And we still occupy and use this land. Many of us spend many months of the year feeding our families from this land. But so much of the land is alienated from us.

In the 1970s the Government of Newfoundland built a huge hydro-electric project that flooded forever the same Mishikamau where our family lived. When Joey Smallwood, premier of Newfoundland, pressed the button to begin flooding, it was a triumphant day for the citizens of Newfoundland, but a sad day for the Innu. Burial grounds, rich hunting territory that sustained us, were destroyed. Even the fish became tainted with methyl-mercury. There was not a word of consultation with us.

From a high spot overlooking a burned area, I saw a black bear. He has a keen sense of hearing, but it was windy. I killed the bear. We hauled the fat carcass back to our camp. We dried the meat and fried the fat to make oil. When it's frozen it looks like lard, but it tastes different . . . it's very good on red berries or on crushed dried meat, or it can be used for candles.

When the lakes freeze, I prepare for winter. I build a storage rack for my canoe. I make my snowshoes and cache/toboggan. Your grandmother makes caribou skin boots for the children and me.

Now each evening we first build a big fire for the children to keep warm before we pitch the tent. In thirty minutes the tent is up and I put in the stove. I still have time to go to the river, make two or three fish holes and put in baited hooks. Next day I had two large "kukamis."

I have a great deal of respect for the Kukamis, our main source of food. Without them I would not be here today.

Not only are areas of our land taken from us, but in the land remaining, our lives are restricted. With no regard for our aboriginal presence, we are subject to many wildlife regulations that prevent us from hunting and fishing. We need licences to hunt the animals that have sustained us for generations. Often we are arrested for "illegal possession of caribou meat," and watch meat, guns and Ski-Doos being seized. At the same time we watch trees being "harvested" for export, lakes becoming private property for sports fishing camps, and trails and roads being cut through land we live on.

With more snow I often had to walk ahead one day to make a path, so that the next day I could pull the toboggan-load of gear, and the children would have less trouble walking.

Gradually we ran out of supplies. There was no more bread to eat, and our tea was the broth from cooking our meat. I could not even smoke while I was hunting, I did not want to waste matches.

We spent two years in Mishikamau Nipi, living on fish and caribou. Mishikamau is about eighty miles long, and twenty to fifty miles wide. Innu walked across in the winter and spring. When we crossed, I hauled firewood on the sled, and halfway across we boiled fish and drank the broth.

We had not seen caribou for a month, our food would not last five days. We made camp in the place where Innu often camped after they had crossed Mishikamau.

I went to the point for dry wood to make a fire before we pitched the tent. On the ice I saw some rocks, but I didn't remember rocks there from other years. It was caribou, eleven of them.

I knew your grandmother was about to start the fire, so I ran back as fast as I could on snowshoes. When she saw me I waved, and she asked what was wrong. I told her there were caribou on the other side of the point. They would have seen the smoke. I did not have to tell her not to light the fire, she already knew.

I walked back through the woods, but they were resting out of range, and I had to wait. It was unusual to see caribou away from the shore, the wolves must have followed them. One was on constant alert, always watching for something to approach them.

I thought about your mother while I was waiting, thinking she must be cold . . . your grandmother must be keeping her warm. Soon one of them got to its feet, and one by one they were all doing the same. They were all stags, without antlers. The one who stood up first must be the leader.

I walked toward the hill they were heading for. I loaded, and when they came within range I shot the leader. The others did not run, and I shot them one by one. I killed eleven. The next day I skinned the caribou and your grandmother dried the meat to make "niueikant."

In 1979, the Government of Canada invited its allies to use the military base, Canadian Forces Base Goose Bay, to conduct low-level training flights. Built during World War II, the base had been another theft of our land, but this low flying was a major increase in the militarization of Nitassinan.

Low-level flying was and still is considered essential for an effective air force, but European citizens were becoming completely unwilling to tolerate these flights over their homes. Exporting the training soothed the citizens and gave far greater flying freedom than ever before. By the late 1980s, the British, Dutch and German air forces were flying nearly eight thousand "sorties" every year during a seven-month flying season.

The Department of National Defence (DND) also constructed a "Practice Target Area," a bombing range where we have seen the huge bomb craters left by metal and concrete bombs. And the DND continues to speak of our land as "ideally suited" for low-level training, because in such a vast space, there is "not one home or permanent residence."

Military officials claim their pilots fly no lower than one hundred feet as they practise terrain-following to underfly enemy radar. But I have seen the jets as low as fifteen to twenty feet, seventeen times in one hour when I was in the country with my family. The noise is devastating, the ground vibrates. And it happens without warning; we do not even have time to protect our children's ears. The startle effect, especially when the flights occur at night, is very frightening for children and elders. At times the children refused to play outside in the daytime, and had difficulty sleeping at night.

In March we started to have mild weather and I decided to go back and get my canoe where we had left it last time. I had to leave very early, around 3:00 a.m., while the snow was still hard. It turned slushy by the middle of the day, and the slush stuck to my snowshoes and could break them. At night I made my own shelter of spruce, and collected enough old tree stumps for firewood. I mixed the dry ones with the wet ones to keep the fire going all night, but by 3:00 in the morning I would be off again. When I reached Mishikamau I hauled my canoe back on my homemade sled.

That summer we canoed along Mishikamau, living on fish and the eggs from ducks and geese. We had not seen any other Innu families. By now they would have gone back to Uashat or Sheshatshit. Since we had not gone back, they probably thought something had happened to us, maybe they considered us dead. But we decided to stay in Mishikamau anyway.

Since these flights began, we can see the destruction. We not only experience the flights, but we observe the animals and fish that are exposed to them. In areas of constant military activity, we have seen dead fish drift ashore, with no external marks on them. We see the thick black exhaust from the jets fall onto the river valleys where they like to fly, and we see the oily film on the water.

We killed four caribou at Kamishtastin Lake. Two were very thin, and when we cleaned the other two, their livers were green in colour, and were sticking to the skin.

The Defence Department contradicts our observations, saying that we Innu are not the "experts." Yet it is not the scientists who have spent months and years on the land, it is us.

These flights must stop. They and the military system that brings them are a serious threat to us and our land.

We stopped on an island about fifty to sixty miles southwest of Mishikamau. There is a stream on the island, and in the stream we saw something unusual. We had never seen rocks glowing. The children played with them, and we examined them. I decided to keep half a sock full of the yellow rocks to show the other Innu families when we meet them.

When we got back to Uashat, our friends were very glad to see that we were alive. A Frenchman, the store manager, must have heard about the rocks we found. He came to see what they were. I showed him and he suggested I show them to another man, who took them. In the fall this man came with a plane and gave us a free trip to Mishikamau in return for the yellow rocks. I guess he wanted me to show him where I found them. But I did not give him anymore. We never saw the person again.

During that time I often wondered why he was so very interested in those yellow stones. But they are flooded now. Mishikamau was all flooded when they built the huge hydro dams on the Mista shipu.

In 1987 much of our resentment and need to fight back showed itself in a community caribou hunt, in defiance of provincial wildlife laws. As we had done for generations, we killed and ate caribou, and many of us were arrested.

It was only the beginning, for we quickly realized that protecting our rights to hunt, protecting our land itself, would be very costly. But we also knew that maintaining the right to hunt was useless if our land was to be turned into bombing ranges and low-level flight corridors.

By this time Goose Bay was buzzing with excitement about a NATO Tactical Weapons Fighter Training Centre. Like earlier hydro dams and mines, it was described as an economic dream-come-true.

We looked at the proposal for thousands of transient servicemen flying forty thousand flights per year, with more bombing ranges and supersonic flight, and we knew the destruction it would bring. We knew it had to be stopped.

We began to occupy the Minai-nipi bombing range, closing it down. Shortly afterwards, over two hundred Innu, old and young, entered the airfield at CFB Goose Bay and walked onto the runway. Our resistance was met with arrests and charges of "mischief." We were seen as trespassers on our own land.

But our actions continued. Many more times we walked on

the runway and occupied the bombing range. And many times men and women spent weeks and months in prison, away from their families. Eventually, several of us were acquitted when an Inuit judge ruled that we honestly believed the land on which we walked was — and is — Innu land. However, this case was thrown out on a technicality, and the group was retried and found guilty.

In the meantime, we started our own court injunction to have the flights stopped, at least until the federal environmental assessment is complete. A federal court judge ruled that the economic blow to Goose Bay residents would be too severe; the flights would continue. To this day, no court ruling stands in support of our efforts to defend our land and life. And the environmental assessment, now in its seventh year, is stalled in the hands of the Defence Department, with no public hearings in sight.

That is how Innu lived. In the 1960s, the government started to build houses for the Innu families, and later they built non-Innu schools. Those Innu families who continued to go into the country at the time were told by the priest to keep their children in the settlement so they could go to school and learn the foreign language, English. So only men went into the country to hunt and trap, leaving their families behind.

In the early 1970s, Innu families hardly went into the country at all and did not travel in the country by foot. Instead, the Innu men, the hunters, chartered a plane.

The Innu mothers received a family allowance from the government if the children attended school. Soon the school hired a truant officer for those who missed school a lot. This English school was very foreign to Innu children.

I remember when your father went to jail in 1972 because you were not going to school. You and me, and the rest of the family spent some time in the country, not very far from the settlement. The priest and the principal came and took you back.

By 1990 some positive signs appeared. Plans for the mammoth NATO Training Centre were cancelled, and at the same time, support for our efforts had grown remarkably in Canada and internationally.

While Defence Department officials continued to talk of the military importance of low flying and the likely increase in flights at Goose Bay, support groups were organizing a major Freedom Walk through central and eastern Canada. People in four provinces were educated about our concerns, and by Remembrance Day, we had reached Ottawa. Well over one hundred people, including five Innu, were arrested for their human blockade of Defence headquarters. Their trials have yet to take place.

We have tried every tactic we can think of, but low-level flights continue. Near the beginning of the Persian Gulf war, the local British air force commander termed his pilots' Goose Bay training as "extremely valuable," for those pilots were in the "front lines" of air force bombardment of Iraq.

We have talked often of the very real connection between preparing for war, and war itself. That connection is very clear today. Innu land was taken and used to prepare for offensive military strikes against Iraq.

In April of 1991 the last of the Innu charged for the resistance actions against the military was tried, and was again found guilty of trespassing. In the same month the Dutch Air Force returned to Goose Bay with sixteen F-16s (a 33 percent increase) and the German Air Force returned with ten F-4s and eight Alpha jets. The British Air Force had not yet recovered from its "activity" in Iraq by that time. Numerous overflights of Innu continue, both inside and outside the areas the DND claims the pilots fly.

For the first time Innu hunters have been given at least a verbal promise that they will no longer be harassed by Newfoundland Wildlife Officers, but only when hunting migratory birds. Wildlife officials have stated that for any other species (which are under provincial jurisdiction, not federal, as with ducks and geese) they will be making arrests and seizures in a "business-as-usual" fashion.

Federal and provincial governments have begun negotiations with the Innu Nation for the purpose of establishing a

Framework Agreement on a Comprehensive Land Claim. However, negotiations have been proceeding very slowly.

We have openly stated that we consider this to be Innu land, that we do not accept the "extinguishment clause" of the federal policy and that we demand a cessation of all developments on our land during the negotiating period. In spite of our misgivings, we have decided to begin this discussion process as yet another way of attempting to protect our land and implement our rights.

By April, dozens of jets will have returned for another seven months of tree-top flight and practice bombing. We know the threat, we have resisted and our resistance shall continue.

I often wonder about the French man in Uashat who gave my grandfather a free trip to Mishikamau because he wanted more gold. Now I understand what the non-Innu are seeking.

PETER PENASHUE

NITASSINAN: NATION TO NATION

The Innu of Nitassinan have been involved for many years in a struggle to stop NATO low-level flying and bombing practices over their land. In 1991 the Innu began comprehensive land claims negotiations with the federal government. When Pierre Cadieux, then Minister of Indian Affairs, met with the community in Sheshatshit, Nitassinan, on June 21, 1989, Peter Penashue, now the President of the Innu Nation, was one of many people to address him in the public meeting.

IT IS A LONG TIME since the people have been given an opportunity to express themselves. When we tried to express ourselves, they put us in jail in St. John's and Stephenville. We are vulnerable and easy to put in jail. We don't have a military. We don't have voting power; we are small in numbers. But we have our honesty. And we have done well with our honesty. We shook Canada; and we shook the House of Commons. A lot of people here have never had the opportunity to express to the oppressor what is happening to them.

My grandfather spoke earlier. I spent a lot of time in the country with him, so I know how he feels. He told me about the incident on Churchill Road (an unpaved, three-hundred-kilometre road running between Goose Bay and Churchill Falls) when his gun was confiscated by a man speaking English, which he doesn't understand. How would you feel if you were on your own land, hunting as you had always done, and as your father and grandfather had done before you, and a man came along speaking a foreign tongue, took away your gun and charged you with doing something illegal?

Mr. Cadieux, you are on Canadian-occupied lands. This situation is no different than that of the people oppressed by Israel. We are a nation, just as the Palestinians are a nation, and you will have to recognize us, just as Israel will have to recognize the Palestinians.

When did we cease to become a nation? When we took your family allowance cheques? I think not. For they are just the crumbs of what you have taken from us.

We are rich in resources. We are rich in humanity. We are real. This is us. We are not here to manipulate you.

I have just come back from St. John's, where the Anglican Church of Canada is holding its General Synod. And I found that there are bishops there who have no consciousness of justice. Their concern is only for the people who support them in their pews. They support the majority. But there were others there, bishops, priests and lay people, who are justice-conscious. And they have heard the concerns of our people.

There is no such thing as democracy here. Where is it? Who gave one nation the right to trample another nation? I think democracy belongs to a nation. As a nation we should determine our own future, just as Canadians should determine their own future. But do it on your own land, not on ours.

I read about the Chinese refugees who are coming here now and begging for refugee status in Canada. But did you come here and ask us for refugee status, for the right to immigrate?

I am going to Japan in August. I have been invited to speak at a conference there about the plight of my people. But I cannot leave my own country without having to falsify a document by saying that I am a Canadian. I asked the woman: "Can I put down Innu nation under nationality?" and she told me: "There's no such country."

Someone told me something about Mary Adele Andrew, one of the elders of the community who occupied the airstrip. He told me that when the RCMP officer took her away at the airstrip, she kept crying: "They threw away the bread . . . they threw away the bread."

I thought about it for the longest time, yet I couldn't understand what she meant by it. But now I do. Jesus ate bread. And Jesus gave us bread as the symbol of his body. Just as that RCMP officer threw away our bread, you threw away a people. You imposed an assimilation process on us that justifies your oppression of us. You have done your work well. Or else why now do our people inflict injuries upon themselves? Why do they beat their children . . . their spouses . . . their neighbours?

In South Africa, although we do not hear that much about it in the media, the Africans have those same problems. They are drinking themselves to hell and beating each other up. That's what oppression does to a people.

You spoke of a dialogue with the Innu, Mr. Cadieux. Do you mean that you are here to talk with us as a father talks with a child? Or are you here for a dialogue between adults?

Do you have a mandate to talk with us as adults? I think not. Do you need that mandate? I think so. I think you would be voted out of your Cabinet if you said, "We have to treat the Innu as adults."

But we have to find ways to make you treat us as adults. You say you will deal with us through the land claims process that has been designed by Cabinet. But that process is a failure. People ask us why we aren't entering the land claims process with the Canadian government. The answer is because it is a failure. It was designed to extinguish our rights, to turn our relationship with the land into a real estate deal.

I am very interested in sitting down with the Canadian government. I am interested because we cannot continue fighting like this. But I am interested in sitting down with you when you are ready; when you are ready to sit down with us as adults. Not when we are ready; when we have finished our land-use and occupancy study [which would put the onus on the Innu to prove the legitimacy of their position]. It's you who should be doing a land-use and occupancy study, not us.

Mr. Cadieux, you have been given the portfolio of working with native groups across Canada. And you have said to us that before we sit down to talk, we have to finish our land use and occupancy study. But we want to sit down to talk about land rights as adults.

We know that the PLO will have to deal with Israel, just as Israel will have to deal with the PLO. And we know it is the same for us. We will have to deal with Canada, just as Canada will have to deal with the Innu.

But we will do it as adult to adult, as nation to nation. Only then can we accomplish justice. Because then we can say, "Let's have low-level flying on the table."

Money does not produce justice. You have the money to solve the Innu's problems, to give us all indoor plumbing and so on. But that will not produce justice.

You do not see it as beneficial for you to deal with us as adults. I know that the U.S. multinational corporations will be in here, ready to spend U.S. dollars on our homelands once you have control of them.

We are very vulnerable, and we hurt. But the Canadian government hurts too. You hurt as well. You don't want to deal with us as the adults we are. But you will deal with us when we have shamed you enough to make you realize that the Innu people are a nation.

REGAINING CONTROL AT FORT GOOD HOPE

THE DENE OF THE NORTHWEST TERRITORIES were not significantly affected by contact with Europeans until the late 1700s. Until then the various families, tribes or nations of Dene were unarguably self-sufficient, self-contained, sovereign peoples with definable land bases and formal economic and political relations with other aboriginal nations.

Through the nineteenth and well into the twentieth century, relations between the Dene/Métis and non-aboriginal peoples occurred within the context of the fur trade. This was primarily an economic relationship rather than a political one. We retained our sovereignty as independent peoples, adjusting, as other nations did, to a more interdependent world. Events like the enactment of the Royal Proclamation of 1763 and the creation of Canada had little consequence in the day-to-day lives of our recent ancestors.

Adapted from "Community and Aboriginal Self-Government in the Northwest Territories: a presentation by the Fort Good Hope Community Council to the Legislative Assembly of the Northwest Territories," October 31, 1989.

Dramatic and significant changes to our status, jurisdiction, economy and lifestyle occurred only when government began to take an active interest in the North. Although the Canadian government had made a unilateral declaration of sovereignty, it did not act on it until prospectors and geologists began to find minerals and oil in our land.

The exploitation of non-renewable resources was not, in the government's view, founded upon principles of mutual dependence. Their primary objective was to secure the economic and, in their view, political right to extract this wealth from the North. The Dene were, first of all, impediments to be removed by way of apparently negotiable, but actually non-negotiable, treaties, and subsequently, fiscal and moral liabilities or "problems" to be addressed through the filtered perceptions of ethnocentrism and paternalism. These developments and attitudes clearly set the stage for the creation of an environment in the North which seriously threatened our economic self-sufficiency, our independence and our ability to effectively govern ourselves and manage our lands.

Even so, it was not until the 1950s, when the government began to actively encourage the Dene/Métis to settle in permanent communities, that a relationship of dependence came to characterize our daily lives. Congregating dispersed and nomadic people at a fixed location made the task of living off the land more difficult. At the same time, settlement life created problems and expectations that required money to address. Only the government had money, and with control over the purse-strings came the power to determine the community's priorities and to set terms and conditions for the expenditure of funds. The Dene/Métis could practise self-government only when they were on the land.

From 1968 to 1977 we resisted the government's plans for our assimilation. We had to oppose the federal government's 1969 White Paper on assimilation; the imposition of foreign institutions of local government, complete with Robert's Rules of Order; and the self-serving colonial slogan, "We're all Northerners." We rejuvenated old institutions like our chiefs and band councils, and we created new ones: the Indian Brotherhood, now the Dene Nation, and the Métis Association.

We successfully spearheaded a campaign to postpone the construction of a Mackenzie Valley pipeline, a project which would have dramatically affected our land and wildlife, our people and communities, and our chances to obtain just recognition of our aboriginal rights.

We succeeded in convincing a justice of the Supreme Court of the Northwest Territories that our aboriginal rights had not been extinguished by the dubious terms of the government's version of our treaties, and that we still retained an undefined interest in our traditional lands. We accomplished this in large part because of the testimony of our elders who were present when the treaty parties met with our leaders in 1899 and 1921.

Finally, the Dene/Métis, our northern neighbours the Inuit and Inuvialuit and other aboriginal nations of Canada, succeeded in convincing the government of Canada that we had aboriginal rights that demanded the negotiation of modern-day treaties, the so-called "comprehensive claims."

These were heady times for us. We truly were reshaping Canadian perspectives and the northern political landscape, and in the process, clarifying and redefining our vision of ourselves.

The period from 1977 to 1981 was not so positive. The Canadian government was determined to regain control over the political agenda.

At the very heart of our aboriginal claim as set forth by our elders was the demand for self-government, coupled with economic self-sufficiency. We felt that if we could govern our lands, we could succeed in governing our lives.

However, the government adamantly insisted that comprehensive claims would deal only with lands and resources, and the Dene/Métis would participate as private parties to an agreement, rather than as self-governing entities. Funds were cut off. Negotiations went nowhere. Threats to terminate the process were made. Eventually we grudgingly agreed to negotiate claims on this basis, but only on the condition that self-government would be addressed in other forums.

In 1981, the Legislative Assembly of the Northwest Territories fought side by side with aboriginal people to ensure that

Canada's original peoples were recognized in the amended Constitution of Canada. In 1983, the leaders of Canada's aboriginal nations sat down with the leaders of the federal and provincial governments to negotiate a further amendment to the Constitution to recognize and entrench our right to self-government.

Unfortunately, by the summer of 1988, when it came time for us to consider accepting an agreement-in-principle as a basis for a final claims settlement, the process initiated at First Ministers' Constitutional Conferences was dead, the constitutional alliance was on hold and there was no prospect for any satisfactory agreement on self-government anywhere on our horizon.

We have not forgotten why we fought so hard to have our aboriginal rights recognized and affirmed. The overriding issue continues to be our right to self-determination, our need to reach an acceptable agreement on aboriginal self-government.

FORT GOOD HOPE: LEAVING HOME

The social and cultural breakdown really began in Fort Good Hope with the opening of the school and hostel in Inuvik in the late 1950s. Many of our school-aged children were sent to Inuvik for most of the year to learn English and other subjects foreign to our way of life. Inuvik was little more than a construction camp, and often our children were affected by the attitudes and behaviour of people accustomed to living in that environment. The children also began to lose their own language, and with it, the ability to communicate with the elders of the community. Family structures began to break down and our language began to suffer. At about the same time, the Indian Act was amended to allow status Dene to drink alcohol.

Despite all these new problems, life around Good Hope was still not too bad. People continued to spend most of their time on the land. They were still, by and large, economically self-sufficient.

Life began to change drastically in the late 1960s. The Indian agent had been replaced by the area administrator. The Northern Rental Housing Program was being introduced to replace the old Indian Affairs log houses. For two dollars a month, people got a house with free oil, water and utilities delivered to their door. There was no need for the regular family chores of hauling water and wood. Welfare and Family Allowance reduced the incentive to travel farther and farther from town to hunt and trap for food and fur. Living in town meant no responsibilities and nothing to do aside from the occasional make-work project. Town life became a destructive environment.

Area administrators were directed by the Department of Local Government to establish Settlement Councils. These new bodies, elected by the community, were supposed to replace the old Advisory Councils, which usually included the local contractor, the Bay manager, the school principal and the priest. The Band Council, on the other hand, had no money and its existence was only acknowledged by government when it was time to distribute $5 bills to each status Dene, according to a treaty arrangement.

By the early seventies, we had come to understand many of the causes of our problems and we were determined to do something about them. Our immediate priorities were to rejuvenate the Band Council; to encourage people to accept responsibility for their situation and to act, to rebuild our families and to get people out of town and back in the bush.

Taking Charge: Inching Closer to Self-Government

There were definite links between the struggles of the Dene/Métis to assert their rights at the national and territorial levels, and our own efforts to regain control over our lands and our futures in Fort Good Hope. Developments beyond our local community helped us to clarify what we had been feeling for a long time but found difficult to articulate and act upon.

Going into the 1970s we had felt we had no power or control, even though we knew our history was being ignored and our own understanding of our rights trampled upon. It was an important psychological breakthrough when Justice Morrow of the Supreme Court of the Northwest Territories ruled that by his law, the law of Canada, our aboriginal land rights continued to exist. It was an even greater breakthrough when another judge, the Honourable Thomas Berger, set our social and political needs and the protection of our land above the interests of big business, big capital and big government in his recommendation of a ten-year moratorium on pipeline construction. Most important of all perhaps, we learned that we could act, that we could have an impact, that we could dare to hope.

In 1973, the Band Council began to take a serious look at the role of the Settlement Council. People who were accustomed to consensus decision making in former times felt left out of the decision process; they didn't like having a few individuals in control. There were too many government boards, committees and councils for government to consult, if they bothered with consultations at all. Government often tried to play off the Band Council, Settlement Council and Métis local against each other, siding with the one which most closely reflected its own view. They were consulting a municipal council rather than our traditional leadership about developments outside the municipality on our traditional lands.

Many of us felt that it was time for us to take responsibility for our own lives, as individuals, as families and as a community. In 1977, only 20 percent of eligible voters bothered to participate in the elections for a Settlement Council. The following year there were no nominations and no one showed up to vote. The government assumed the task of providing municipal services; but they no longer had the body they wanted to use to represent the public interest.

We got on with the business of building our own community government. People began to work with the band through a series of public meetings. In order to help bring us closer together, we redefined our band to include all descendants of the Dene, including Métis, although we appreciated there were reasons to retain a Métis local in our community for certain purposes. We increased the size of our Band Council to ten to accommodate the new members.

Representation for non-aboriginal residents was not really an issue because nearly all were in Good Hope only for the purposes of their current employment and they intended to leave as soon as their employment status changed. There were no non-aboriginal children in our school.

In 1977, we passed a motion that no more rental housing would be built in Fort Good Hope. In 1978, we passed a plebiscite to prohibit alcohol in our community. In 1982, we created a Community Assembly which included all adult residents of Good Hope. The Assembly had the authority to make all the important decisions for the community. The role of the Community Council was to implement those decisions.

Eventually we drafted a charter, or constitution, which described our system of community self-government, and reached a contractual understanding with the Department of Local Government, whereby we would assume responsibility for the provision of municipal services.

But we had done much more than simply put municipal services into the hands of the Good Hope Band. We had created, with the thoughtful participation of many band members over an extended period of time, a system of community self-government we were comfortable with; one which we felt would properly and accurately represent our interests.

ROADBLOCKS TO SELF-GOVERNMENT

Our serious problem continues to be in the area of jurisdiction; the kinds and amount of authority the Community Assembly and Council can exercise, with and on behalf of our people. While the government now recognizes our community government as the representative of our community, it still only recognizes it as having authority for municipal services, and it merely *consults* the Council on other matters.

Perhaps we should have gone around to every other government department — Education, Economic Development, Housing, Justice, Health and Social Services — and negotiated contractual agreements the same way we negotiated with local government. But this should not be necessary. We are a community government, not a private corporation. We should not be receiving our authority by contract.

What we require is legislation that recognizes our authority as public and aboriginal governing bodies for the setting of policy and the delivery of programs and services at the community level so we can do so in a manner that is suitable to our particular needs and aspirations.

Important elements of community self-government are: being allowed to create a structure and system of local government that makes sense to local residents; and having the power, authority and resources to address the needs of our residents on a day-to-day basis without constantly having to depend on, persuade and adjust our priorities to satisfy bureaucrats in Yellowknife.

One of the most important areas of community jurisdiction that remains undefined is the community's interest in community lands beyond the boundaries set for municipal purposes. When the people of Fort Good Hope talk about community lands, they are invariably referring to all the lands in the vicinity of Good Hope and Colville Lake that local residents have been using for many years for traditional economic pursuits.

We have been seeking recognition of our jurisdiction over these lands for almost twenty years. Our goal has always been to protect our lands and ensure local benefits by controlling development.

When we speak of owning our traditional lands, we mean that we continue to have jurisdiction over what happens on or under it. The selection in claims negotiations of certain lands for private title does not constitute a relinquishment of our political interests in the region.

Perhaps the most critical element in the self-government process is to find satisfactory ways to recognize our right to exercise control over our land locally in a manner that complements our participation in a territorial jurisdiction.

This issue highlights the distinction between "aboriginal self-government" and "community self-government." In our view, these lands are aboriginal lands, not public lands, and the control should rest with aboriginal people, not with numerous departments of the federal or provincial governments.

OIL AND GAS EXPLORATION: WHO'S THE BOSS?

The events of the last decade will illustrate the difficulties we have encountered because of this clash of views, as well as the distance we have managed to travel.

A number of oil companies obtained rights to oil and gas, and land-use permits to do exploration work on our lands, in the 1970s. We became concerned that Good Hope had no authority over the companies or their permits, that the community and residents experienced various negative effects and very little benefit, and that much of our land was being alienated or otherwise compromised before our claims were settled.

In 1980, the Dene succeeded in obtaining from the Honourable John Munro, then Minister of Indian Affairs, a freeze on all further leases for oil and gas exploration in Denendeh. However, companies who obtained their leases before the freeze came into effect continued to work in our area for some time. Our community continued to negotiate with the Minister of Indian Affairs, and by October 1983, we had succeeded in securing an Interim Land Use Procedures Agreement with the federal government. Our goal was to try to create a land-use management regime that required community screening. We also wanted to have our land base defined so that the agreement would acknowledge and apply to all of Good Hope's and Colville Lake's hunting, trapping and fishing areas. We succeeded on both these points and secured additional clauses dealing with employment, contracts, environmental monitoring and compensation to traditional land users for damages or losses caused by exploration work.

By that time the old leases had expired. In early 1983, British Petroleum (BP) was conducting some speculation surveys on our land, an activity that did not require a lease. The Band and BP developed a working relationship and agreed to try to design an exploration project that would include the community of Fort Good Hope and Colville Lake as full partners.

At first we considered only the economic issues as part of the agreement, but were not satisfied with the results. Then we started to explore the possibilities for joint management. This was very attractive to us because it represented an opportunity to extend our authority over our lands. Eventually we worked out a comprehensive agreement with British Petroleum that included employment, training, joint ownership, a management regime and a definition of the relationship between BP and the community of Good Hope. The agreement would operate within Good Hope's definition of its traditional land base.

We made a point of consulting with the Dene and Métis Assemblies to ensure that our agreement would not jeopardize claims negotiations with the federal government in any way. We also wanted to make clear the relationship between the Dene/Métis *national* interest and our aboriginal *community* interest. The national interest involved a share of the revenues from the project; the community interest had to do with ownership and control of the lands in question, and the employment, contract and revenue benefits that accrue to the community.

Then we went directly to the federal government and requested them to issue a land-use permit to BP on the basis of our agreement and the community's overall approval of the project. This was a radical departure from the usual way in which government granted land-use permits to oil companies. Usually the community was the last and the least important step in the issuance of a permit. At best a community would be consulted, though its opinions were seldom reflected in the final plan.

Officials of Canada Oil and Gas Lands Administration (COGLA) were upset. They saw the evaluation of proposals and the issuance of leases as their private domain. They hated the idea of a community and an oil company reaching a satisfactory arrangement without them. Their procedures called for the use of public tenders, with exploration rights generally being granted to the highest bidder.

The Canadian Petroleum Association was upset too. They demanded the conventional public tender to solicit bids and they were strongly opposed to the direct issuance of a lease. Officials of the government of the Northwest Territories were also unhappy. They wanted to be the ones negotiating with oil companies and the federal government.

David Crombie, the Minister for Indian Affairs, was prepared to approve our deal, but COGLA and the Canadian Petroleum Association succeeded in changing his mind. We finally accepted the tender approach, but only on the condition that our comprehensive criteria be used to assess each application. The Honourable Pat Carney, Minister of Energy, Mines and Resources, accepted our proposal. "Trust me," she told us at our meeting in Inuvik, "It will all work out."

The tenders went out based on our community criteria, but the highest bidder criteria was included. Fort Good Hope wanted to have the Dene/Métis included on the selection team, but this never happened. Instead, we met with the selection team, COGLA, plus one official of the Department of Indian Affairs and Northern Development and one government of NWT official, and carefully explained our needs and interests.

The team then proceeded to select Chevron over BP and the other applicants. We were enraged. We couldn't believe it. Chevron had never spoken to us and could not possibly have matched BP's offer, which was based on the negotiated recognition of our needs and interests. We were convinced that the only factor the selection team had taken seriously was the highest bid.

Fort Good Hope and BP objected. In implementing his predecessor's freeze on new leases, the Honourable David Crombie had promised us that Good Hope could veto any applicant approved by the selection team for this permit. While this gave us considerable influence over the process, it was a power we wanted to exercise only as a last resort. A number of public and private officials had argued that the Dene/Métis were anti-development and that the government and the public could not trust power in the hands of aboriginal people. A premature veto by Good Hope on this project might have given them more ammunition for the next round.

However, aside from this external pressure, it is important to remember that we had voluntarily entered into the original agreement with BP because we supported development in our region so long as our rights were respected, our land was protected and the people of our region would benefit.

We were determined to try to salvage a fair deal from what appeared to be another classic example of bad faith on the part of big government towards small communities and aboriginal people. Once it became obvious that we could not reinstate BP's proposal, we offered to negotiate a similar deal with Chevron.

In late 1986, the new Minister of Indian Affairs, Bill McKnight, agreed to this approach. Three years had passed since we had negotiated the interim land-use procedures agreement, three and a half years since negotiations began with BP, and six years since we had secured a freeze on all new leases. What an incredible waste of time and money! So much could have been accomplished in a much shorter time frame if government had simply acknowledged our shared jurisdiction over our traditional lands and negotiated accordingly.

The first six months of discussions with Chevron were a repeat of the negotiations with BP, a form of "cross-cultural workshop" as each party gradually came to appreciate the other's needs and aspirations. Once this was accomplished, it took us a mere two months, until June 1987, to reach a Joint Venture Agreement with Chevron very similar to the one we had originally negotiated with BP. The only significant difference was the reduced size of the community's equity in the project.

Our joint venture has worked out very well for both Chevron and the community. Whenever problems arise, we work them out within the context of our agreement. The work is proceeding under our joint management, many of our residents have received training and employment, the environment has been monitored and protected, and the community's equity in the project grows each year. Chevron, for its part, has been able to accomplish its objectives confident that it has the support of the people. Government has had nothing to complain about either.

However, it is important not to forget that our agreement with Chevron, despite its comprehensive and public nature, takes the form of a contract between private parties. Even though it recognizes our traditional land base and involves us in all decision making, it is limited to this one project, and it is not formulated on the basis of Fort Good Hope and Colville Lake having a universally recognized, formal jurisdiction over our traditional lands.

The Interim Land Use Procedures Agreement of 1983, which recognizes our land base and includes us in decision making, is still in effect, but its survival is dependent upon the continued goodwill and good faith of the minister. We were unsuccessful in attempts to renegotiate certain terms of this agreement (on the matter of "consultation," for example). The federal response was that this was an issue for claims negotiations, and thus a matter for the various boards described in the claims agreement in principle.

A NEW VISION

The federal government's response was inappropriate because we are talking about political rights and jurisdiction, not private land rights or compensation. This is clearly an outstanding issue of community and aboriginal self-government, and it is a major element in our constitutional proposals to the NWT Legislative Assembly.

Our proposals lay out the parameters of "community self-government," which refers to the local government of all bona fide residents of a community, and "aboriginal self-government" in the Northwest Territories, which gives jurisdiction to aboriginal peoples as groups, within and in conjunction with the various levels of government.

The proposal features the creation of "cultural caucuses," which would recognize the distinct cultural interests and values of different groups including "northerners" (those who have moved to the North from elsewhere). It would be possible to "join" a different cultural community if a person felt more comfortable with that community's collective values. Each cultural community would have a number of seats (at local and territorial levels of government) based on its proportion of the total population, although an elected representative wouldn't need to be a member of that cultural group. Thus there would be a mechanism for representing group concerns of fundamental importance when that is called for.

In our proposal we have endeavoured to acknowledge the fundamental reality of northern society. We recognize the original peoples of the North — the Dene, Métis, Inuvialuit and Inuit — as unique and distinct peoples possessing recognized constitutional rights as well as a common desire to continue to develop as self-governing peoples within the context of a complex northern society.

But we have also acknowledged the presence of another group of people who plan to make the North their home for a few years or indefinitely. We do not pretend that each of these groups has the same interests or that non-aboriginals have all the rights of people whose ancestors have known no other home. But we do believe it is possible and, given the right environment, even desirable that our cultural communities can come together and reach a general consensus on the future of the North and each community's respective place within it.

We believe our proposals bridge that gap, that their implementation would bring our respective peoples together in a manner that encourages confidence and respect: promoting self-confidence and self-respect, and confidence in and respect for each other.

By feeling secure in the knowledge that each of us will play an important role in shaping the North as well as shaping ourselves, we can afford to trust each other. We can afford to explore options of mutual interest in ways that, to date, we have been unable to entertain.

This is what northern society should be about. This is the environment we want to help create.

WALDEMAR BRAUL

INGENIKA POINT:
NO MORE RIVERBOATS

IMAGINE GETTING LOST in your own country!"
This was the reaction of Ingenika elder Jean Isaac in 1971 as she travelled by barge on the new Williston Reservoir. Three years earlier, most of her homeland had been flooded to make way for a hydro-electric power project.

The Williston Reservoir forever changed the lives of the Ingenika people. Before the flood, the Ingenika were an independent and self-sufficient people, relying on their traditional livelihoods of hunting, fishing and trapping. But the economic and cultural sustenance of the Ingenika people was deemed expendable by the provincial government in order to provide power to British Columbia's lower mainland. The flood came without warning, let alone consultation or compensation.

The Ingenika, or Tsay Keh Dene ("people of the mountain") have, since time immemorial, lived in and around the valleys of the Ingenika River and many other rivers in north-central B.C., an area now flooded by the reservoir. They are one of three groups that make up the Sekani Nation.

Anyone visiting the Ingenika community would soon conclude that the people are "ordinary folk," good neighbours. Conversations here centre on jobs, kids, hockey and the Vancouver

Canucks, the weather and the health of parents. There are also some extraordinary discussions about new beginnings. The starting point for these discussions is always the reservoir: it daily symbolizes the life-and-death implications of politics and law. The Ingenika people are acutely aware of what happens when Canada's political and economic institutions fail.

The story of the flooding of Ingenika land and the devastation it caused is ultimately the story of the resilience of the Ingenika people, their reliance on their homeland, their hard work to keep their community intact against all odds, and their unwavering hope for establishing a new constitutional basis for harmonious native–non-native relations.

British Columbia's Legacy of Conflict

Before contact with Europeans, the Ingenika elders say, their ancestors hunted, fished, trapped and gathered in seasonal cycles, travelling in relatively small groups of several families over extensive areas.[1]

The Sekani first experienced the indirect influence of European exploration in the late 1700s. Captain James Cook established contact on the West Coast in 1778, and an east-west pattern of trade extended into Sekani territory. The Sekani nation actively participated in this trading network, first with intermediary First Nations, and later directly when explorers travelled up the Peace River. The Sekani valued the new goods — beads, guns, and iron — that trade brought. In fact, at least for the first decades of the nineteenth century, the fur trade seemed mutually beneficial. First Nations were still free to choose which aspects of European culture to incorporate into their own.[2]

The fur trade economy of the late eighteenth and early nineteenth centuries was supported by British Crown policy. The British sought to maintain friendship with the First Nations, because they could not afford more enemies. In their struggle for control in North America, the British shrewdly recognized that the loyalty of strong First Nations was essential for military control and good business. Not surprisingly, the British Crown expressly recognized native nations and aboriginal rights in the Royal Proclamation of 1763.

The European–native coexistence began to erode with the influx of miners in Sekani territory when gold was found in the Upper Peace River in 1861. By 1897, several thousand gold-hungry miners were swarming through Sekani country on the way to the Klondike. The B.C. government granted licences, leases or outright land ownership for revenue — an administratively simple method of tapping the immense natural resource wealth. This regulatory system is still the central principle of a number of B.C. laws, such as the Forest Act and the Land Act.

At no time did the regulatory system recognize native interests, a fact that has led to untold conflict between the Sekani and European settlers and miners for the past century or more. Nor were such conflicts addressed by the 1871 Terms of Union with the rest of Canada which brought B.C. into Confederation. The Terms were silent on how aboriginal interests should be incorporated within provincial legislation, and accordingly, were interpreted by the province, until only recently, to mean that aboriginal interests did not exist. It was this interpretation, in fact, that triggered the first provincial–federal constitutional crisis. When the province first passed the Land Act in 1874, the federal government, using its constitutional power, disallowed the Act because it failed to expressly address the "Indian interest." The crisis was later resolved (1876), at least as far as the two governments were concerned, when the federal government relented, opening the door for more provincial legislation free of any consideration of how to deal with the First Nations.

The new province, as a matter of policy, chose not to enter into treaties prior to resource development. This policy contrasts with that of the federal government, which entered into the so-called "numbered treaties" across the prairies. It also contrasts with the policy of the pre-Confederation colonial administration under Governor James Douglas which entered into several treaties on Vancouver Island. In the late 1800s, the province resisted vigorous lobbying by First Nations calling on the province to enter into treaties that set out the basic terms of native–non-native relations and land ownership. The Sekani Nation has never signed a treaty.

ESTABLISHING RESERVES

In 1916, the McKenna-McBride Commission, established by the federal and provincial governments to allot reserves throughout B.C., created two reserves near Fort Grahame for Sekanis who frequented the fort. Initially, the allotment of the Fort Grahame reserve did not alter the Sekani lifestyle to any great degree. The Sekanis continued to use Fort Grahame and many other spots as their bases, and continued their traditional livelihoods. As the Ingenika band chief said in a 1984 interview:

> In those days I don't think our people even knew who the government was or what the government did for the people. They had no idea there was a sort of form of government out in the world. They just made their own living and did not depend on anybody. They were very independent, our people, and they were proud of what they did and who they were and how they provided for their families.

The Commission's work reflected the government's haphazard attitude towards consulting with native people. It failed to recognize, for example, that although the band traded at Fort Grahame and maintained several houses at the fort for summer use, their more important and permanent settlement was at Finlay Forks, fifty miles south. The Commission's oversight was not surprising, given that the only consultation with the band was a chance meeting with a Sekani hunting expedition and little more than a chat with the government's Indian agent from Burns Lake, which is well outside Sekani territory.

WILLISTON RESERVOIR

In the late 1950s, the province of British Columbia took the first step to harness Peace River power by commissioning a study on the potential of hydro development. The formal decision to go ahead was made in 1963, and by 1968 BC Hydro had completed the project. It consisted of the W.A.C. Bennett Dam, the Shrum power station, and the Williston Reservoir. The power project produced almost half of B.C.'s electricity in 1970 and now yields approximately one quarter of B.C.'s electricity. The Williston Reservoir is B.C.'s largest body of water.

The reservoir flooded the Ingenika's Fort Grahame reserves, other homes in many river valleys, many of the best trapping and hunting areas, cemeteries and other culturally significant spots, and main rivers such as the Finlay, which had served as transportation corridors. The reservoir destroyed the best valleys — the heart of the Ingenika people's ancestral territories.

Ingenika elders explain that the government made virtually no attempt to consult with the Ingenika people before the flood. They do not recall, for instance, any meetings with the B.C. Government, BC Hydro, or the Department of Indian Affairs to discuss the project. Some elders recall a BC Hydro summer student, a year or two before the flood, telling whomever he met that the valley was to be flooded. Other elders recall that several BC Hydro and Department of Indian Affairs officials held sporadic conversations with the band members they happened to meet. One elder says the officials told him the flood would reach the "250 level," jargon that would surely be useless to anyone but Hydro engineers. No one explained what the reservoir would look like. There was little information about compensation or how the bands might legally oppose the project. To make matters worse, many band members did not even understand English.

In the superficial contact that did take place, the Ingenika people spoke out clearly against the project. Maggie Pierre stated in 1984:

> Dad was completely against the flooding. He saw survey guys, and he told them, "How would you feel if I went to the city

and started hanging ribbons all over the place and told you that was for smashing down your houses?"

Prior to the flood, the Department of Indian Affairs promised to compensate band members for loss of traplines and trapping equipment. A number of members were promised payments of between $1000 and $2500 for their losses. Band members say they were told these amounts were to compensate them for one year, and that there would be further talks to discuss further compensation once the reservoir level had been determined. The Department has never returned to talk, however. Indeed, many band members say they have never received even the initial amounts.

One of the first clear warnings of the flood was when the government burned band members' cabins. Elder Francis Isaac remembers how he had travelled up the Finlay River just before the flood, and found many cabins, with their contents, burned to the ground. These cabins, the band members later learned, were located below the "250 level." After this week-long heart-breaking trip, Francis Isaac went back to Finlay Forks to tell people what had been done. There was no compensation for the levelled homes.

When the flood water rose in 1967 and 1968, band members did not know how high it would go. To their horror, they watched the reservoir go far beyond their expectations. Elders describe how they moved their camps and homes up the sides of the valley, only to move them again and again before the water reached the "250 level." Francis Isaac describes some of the immediate effects of the flood:

> One time we were coming up Five Mile [Creek] and we heard a moose calling. Here a bull moose was caught under a tree. We chopped at it, but by the time we got it loose he had already drowned. A moose calf was nearby and we brought it to shore. . . . we used to even rescue squirrels, bring them to dry land.

The cruel irony of the burned cabins discovered by Francis

Isaac is that the government thought it necessary to burn down homes, but did not bother to cut the valley timber before the flood, leaving years of harvestable timber on the reservoir bottom. As the submerged timber decayed, it rose to the surface; approximately 1800 acres of the surface of the reservoir was covered with floating logs in 1968. The debris impeded and often prevented travel by boat, and much of it remains to this day. Band member Elsie Pierre describes the problem:

> Mom and them want to go across the reservoir trapping, but they can't. Used to be all they had to do was cross the river. Almost all the riverboats have been smashed because of wind and logs. Now none of us has boats, hardly anyone uses boats because they will probably lose them again.

There were few government engineers to watch the flood's devastation. One non-native onlooker, Bill Bloor, former owner of the general store at Finlay Forks, remembers this scene:

> One evening as the waters were coming up, I went over to where the natives were. They had camp-fires lit, all in a row. They were seated around these camp-fires. It was as though I had come to a funeral. Like a vigil, they were watching what was happening. The older people were weeping. They were saying, "No more good land." They knew it was no longer safe. It was a very, very sorrowful sight.

In fact, the creation of the reservoir has had worse consequences than anyone expected. It serves as a grim daily reminder of one of B.C.'s greatest ecological blunders. The reservoir water is undrinkable, likely the result of the rotting of timber left in the reservoir. Band members see new diseases in the declining fish catches. And like ghosts that continue to haunt, twenty-year-old floating logs still clutter large portions of the reservoir, creating a threat to people venturing onto the water with anything short of a tugboat. High winds now create dust storms from the newly deposited silt, causing eye and respiratory problems for many members of the community. In addition, BC

Hydro causes the reservoir level to fluctuate by up to forty feet, and is allowed to do so without warning.

MACKENZIE RESERVES

In 1968, the federal government established two replacement reserves near the new town of Mackenzie, some one hundred miles south of the Ingenika River, well outside the band's traditional territory. Government officials made superficial efforts, at most, to consult with the Ingenika people about the new reserves. They selected and then proposed two sites that the band had never seen. Records of the few meetings that did occur show that the Ingenika people had little say in choosing a replacement for their flooded Fort Grahame reserve; the sites proposed for "approval" appeared to be a "take it or leave it" offer.

The bands were expected to abandon their traditional economy overnight. The officials no doubt assumed that the new reserves would provide ready access to work at the new pulp mill and sawmill in Mackenzie. (Ironically, the Mackenzie mills used timber from Ingenika territory, now made accessible to tugboats and barges by the reservoir.) But jobs were unavailable, as were trapping opportunities. Land was either being logged or was occupied by other native bands. One member who tried to make his home at the new reserve remembers:

> It had good houses, washers, running water, but I don't think so much of that place. You couldn't get a job there — I tried all over. The mill was going, but you couldn't get a job anywhere. And we couldn't trap there.[3]

Only alcohol, and not employment, became more accessible to the band, and for the first time, alcohol began to afflict the community.

Not surprisingly, most members did not even bother to make the long trip to the Mackenzie reserves. When the waters rose in 1967 and 1968, some stayed near Finlay Forks, some moved to Ingenika Point, and others located up and down the unflooded portions of their territory.

REBUILDING THE COMMUNITY AT INGENIKA POINT

Those who did go to the Mackenzie reserves realized early on that something had to be done. They knew they had no future if they remained next to the pulp mill. Their lives were based on their homelands, even if these lands were only remnants. In the summer of 1971, some fifty or sixty members moved to Ingenika Point, a high point of land where the Ingenika River once flowed into the Finlay River. Since then, the Mackenzie reserves have stood empty.

Jean Isaac describes the journey back to Ingenika Point:

When we moved back up here from Finlay Forks, we came on the barge; long ride — one night and half a day. Pretty dangerous with so many kids; windy day too. Francis, myself and Bessie went with Billy Van Somers' riverboat. We took our children with us; they were small then. We got lost at the Ospika. Imagine getting lost in your own country. It became windy; we had to crowd in the back of the boat to keep above the waves. We could hardly even recognize our own country. That's the first time after the flood we took a boat up to Ingenika. After that we could hardly get around anymore because our riverboats were too small.

As traumatic as it was, the trip back to Ingenika Point was probably the easiest step in rebuilding the community. Many other challenges were to follow. One immediate task was to reorganize trap lines. The best trapping areas had been flooded, and establishing new trap lines meant adapting to higher, less productive land.

Another immediate concern was to obtain reserve status for the new settlement at Ingenika Point. One would think that, as a minimal gesture, the provincial or federal government would readily establish new reserves at Ingenika Point. But the fight to obtain reserves took almost two decades. The people were told by government officials that they were "squatting" on Crown land, with a veiled threat that they could be evicted. Reserve status, while not a total solution, was seen by the band as providing a measure of security. The land would at least be recognized by the government as belonging to the band, and the community could then plan ahead and establish schools and other community facilities.

Finally, in early 1989, the people decided to bring their story to Vancouver. The Ingenika story was carried by newspapers, television and radio. As a result, politicians finally went to the negotiating table. Within months of the media blitz, a deal was signed.

Today the Ingenika people live on a new reserve site, chosen by them, with new houses for all families (built mostly by band members) and community facilities. The band has also decided to develop a stronger base for a modern "wage economy." After the flood, the community could no longer rely on trapping as an economic base. In recent years, the band, local forest companies and the provincial government have undertaken a joint venture allowing the band to undertake logging. Local forestry is, however, a two-edged sword; in the band's experience, it has destroyed wildlife habitat, and yet has provided few jobs. The band recognizes the dilemma it faces and has prepared a community plan that seeks the right balance between traditional and modern wage economies. The resolve to create a viable future is reflected by a comment by Chief Pierre before the reserve agreement:

We know what we want. There will be a village right here [indicating the site of the new reserve]. It will have modern facilities: water, a school, maybe even a community hall — the whole works. By then, we may have arranged to manage [forestry]. I'd like to see young guys in business for themselves. . . . I'm really pushing education so they can do that. . . . A whole generation lost education because of the flood. We're just starting all over again for the young kids.

Along with the exhausting struggle to re-establish a reserve and ongoing attempts to develop the modern side of their economy, the band has been fighting a number of rearguard actions. The band is currently participating in a review of a lead-zinc mine proposed by Curragh Mines, to be located about twenty-five kilometres from the new reserve site. The mine would employ several hundred people. The band is concerned about water pollution, acid mine drainage and loss of wildlife habitat. Two years ago, the band fought another development proposal, this time a provincial initiative to grant tree farm licences to large forestry corporations. The band succeeded in arguing that the holders of tree farm licences would dominate decision making in the local forests and prejudice the settlement of land claims; the proposal was eventually abandoned. Needless to say, the band's energy is stretched to the limit when dealing with megaprojects that seem to come out of the blue.

SELF-GOVERNMENT

The Ingenika people now face the challenge of creating a system of self-government that enables them to regain self-sufficiency. Self-government and self-sufficiency, however, ultimately depend on land rights. This is nothing new; it has been asserted by the Sekanis and other First Nations since the first days of contact with non-natives. In 1984, the Sekani Nation, in conjunction with the Carriers, their neighbours to the south, launched a comprehesive land claim to ancestral lands. The claim asserts, in part, that the Crown has broken its promises to protect unceded Indian lands.

It won't be easy to achieve the goal of self-government. Long-standing mining and forestry "rights" granted to the many resource developers will require compensation if land claim agreements involve the transfer of land rights back to the First Nations. Needless to say, aboriginal land claims have been, and will continue to be, strongly resisted, or at least hotly contested, by government.

Like many other bands, the Ingenika people are seeking

protection from Canada's Constitution to prevent land claims agreements from being undone unilaterally by a future government. The constitutional protection of self-government should provide the basic framework from which to assess resource projects. The band should not be expected to fight resource developers and the Crown at every turn.

The drama of the Ingenika story illustrates that politics, economics and constitutional law are, at least for native people, life-and-death matters. For the Ingenika people, governmental mechanisms — both the conventional legal and political systems and new forms of self-government — are seen as building blocks for constructing their community. Self-government may breathe new life into Confederation. The story of the Williston Reservoir and the determination of the Ingenika to rebuild their community is not just their story; it is part of British Columbia's history, albeit a part that is not well known or happily told. By sharing their story — and reliving a great deal of pain as a result — the Ingenika people hold out hope for beginning a new and more harmonious chapter in the history of British Columbia.

ELSIE FIDDLER

FROM CEDAR LAKE TO EASTERVILLE: MOURNING FOR WHAT MY PEOPLE LOST

T HE GROWN-UPS ASSEMBLED and spoke in hushed tones. There was a feeling in the air that something terrible had happened or was about to happen. Gradually . . . bit by bit . . . I started to learn that our whole community was being moved to a different site.

I couldn't help but feel excited at the thought of moving. I couldn't understand why so many people were speaking out against it. After all, if we didn't like our new home, we could always return to Cedar Lake.

The people were packing everything they owned in boxes and one by one, they were being put on the big boat to be taken to the new site. I felt so left out, and feared being left behind.

My grandparents were not doing a thing to prepare for the move. My grandmother still insisted we were not going anywhere. My grandfather still read his Bible every day and I know he felt God would help him.

This article originally appeared in the October 15, 1990 issue of *Anglican Magazine*.

They both spoke of a dam in Grand Rapids and of this thing called Manitoba Hydro. But I really didn't understand what it was all about. Maybe it would be something good because they said Manitoba Hydro would give us a whole bunch of money, just for moving away. I couldn't understand why some people didn't want to accept good money and leave. I would have.

One day a man from Grand Rapids came to see my grandparents. He talked in glowing terms of the developments in Grand Rapids — a new hotel, new stores, nice houses and roads.

He talked of a road going all the way to Winnipeg and of how some people had cars. As he lit his pipe, he talked about flipping a switch on the wall and he could make tea or cook a meal.

My Aunt Ida remarked: "I bet they even plug in his pipe and he doesn't need a match." How we laughed at that one.

Some time later a family member came to our house. My brothers and I were playing outside, unaware that our futures were being debated inside in angry tones. My grandfather hardly ever raised his voice in anger, but there was no mistaking the fury in his voice that day. Granny, oh, my poor, dear grandmother, was crying softly.

Their visitor came out and as he walked away, he reminded them: "Don't forget, if you refuse to leave, these children will be taken away."

My brother Roy and I were living with our grandparents and I knew they wouldn't let them take us away. When I heard those words I promised my brother that if we were given away, if I ever had a baby boy, I would call him Roy.

From that day on, we waited for the Mounties to show up and take us away. In my young mind, I formed a mental picture of Mounties being like the soldiers on horseback that I saw at the picture show. I wondered if they would hang us right there or shoot us, if we made a run for it.

In an effort to feel secure, I made several bows and stocked up on arrows. For good measure, I made a slingshot. All these preparations were done without anybody's knowledge and to this day, my weapons remain buried where I stored them.

The Mounties never did come, but eventually my grandparents made a half-hearted effort to pack all their belongings. They admitted defeat, but their spirits were still very much alive.

Finally, the day came when we boarded the big boat and got ready to sail to our new home. As we pulled away from the dock, we sat in the boat, facing backwards, and I will never forget the pain etched in Granny's face. As she placed her fist in her mouth to stifle her sobs, she held me closer.

Somehow I understood. That day, in my grief and anger at seeing my grandmother hurting so, I swore I would never forgive whoever was doing this to her.

On our arrival in Easterville, we were met by Walter and Clara Hart. They took us to their house for a meal and Walter did his best to convince my grandparents they'd made a smart move.

They were excited about their new home, but now I was starting to get really scared. I felt like I didn't know anybody and there was no sign of green grass anywhere. At Cedar Lake, I had enjoyed visiting with my friends while sitting on the grass. We spent many an hour lying on the grass, reading or just passing the time. Now it was starting to look like that part of my life was gone forever.

Finally we were settled in the home of my cousin and his wife. Besides himself and his wife and three sons, he also had his parents, two brothers, my grandparents, my mother, my aunt, my four brothers and myself to contend with — all under one roof.

Because we were so busy just trying to find a place to sit down, I felt alone and neglected. My cousin had married earlier that year, so I couldn't expect her to entertain me. I felt out of sorts and cried a lot that summer.

Sensing my urgent need for some companionship, Granny told me that I could go and find my Uncle Adam's house the next day.

Early the next morning, I set out. In spite of the rain, I was determined to find my cousins that day. As I was sliding in the mud and trying to keep my balance, I seemed to be going around in circles. I was soaked to the skin and shivering from the cold by then. I decided to go back, and when I turned around I slipped and fell to my knees in the mud. It was then that I finally gave in to my agony and frustration and cried bitter tears of regret and anger.

I headed towards my cousin's house, where we were living,

and decided that I would tell Granny we should all go home soon to Cedar Lake.

A week later we were given a new house and it was neat and smelled of fresh paint. I didn't unpack, as I knew we were going home soon. Eventually, I got tired of waiting and brought up the subject of our return. It was then Grandpa told me we were never going home. I remember turning away from him in hurt and anger, vowing that the first chance I got, I was gone from Easterville.

Life sort of settled into a comfortable routine, but deep within, I sensed an uneasiness, a longing for something I couldn't fathom.

One day there was a hum of excitement in the air and my own mother came home, waving a cheque from Manitoba Hydro. It was a form of payment for moving away from Cedar Lake, and people referred to the payments as "pollution cheques." Considering what the cheques were used for, I guess pollution is the word for it.

The arrival of these cheques introduced me to a frightful new experience — the use of alcohol. Back at Cedar Lake, I had heard of people drinking home brew and staggering when they tried to walk. I had never actually seen this, although I remember one Christmas when two brothers from another reserve got into a fight and we heard the noise they made. They were screaming and swearing. From that, I judged that getting drunk wasn't a good thing.

But to actually see people walking around with beer bottles in their hands and not looking or acting like themselves was unbelievable. I didn't know how to deal with this new development.

The year of our move, I was in the eighth grade in school and looked forward to quitting as soon as I passed. I was always curious as to what went on at home while we were away at school. Now this great mystery would be revealed.

My teacher really encouraged me and towards the end of the year, started talking about my going away to school. I didn't make any plans and I just let him think I was receptive to the idea.

My friend and classmate was all set to go. She and I were the only ones in the eighth grade and I felt happy for her to be going away to school.

Then one night my mother brought a man over and introduced him to everyone. He had a bottle of wine with him and my aunt and Mom joined him in a drink. I only hoped they wouldn't get drunk. But then my grandfather accepted a glass of wine and how that hurt me.

I retired into my room and cried for hours afterwards until my throat started to burn. Early the next morning I was at school, telling my teacher I was prepared to go away to school.

It wasn't until years later that I realized my grandparents were acting that evening, hoping to provoke me into that decision.

It was time to leave home for school. I was so lonely when I got to Cranberry Portage that I wrote home and told everyone I was miserable. Grandpa wrote and said why didn't I stay until Thanksgiving?

Come Thanksgiving, he misplaced his wallet, so he couldn't send me the money for bus fare. He'd never borrow from Granny.

Anyway, Christmas was coming, so I could come home then. But when I got home, they said it was very cold in our new house and I'd be better off living where there was electric heat.

So back I went, with a promise that I could quit at Easter time. Easter came and went. I went back to school till June. At Easter, they had decided that since I was so close to the end of the school year, why didn't I finish grade nine? It would be something to be proud of. That was how I got through my first year of high school away from home.

Today, I refer lovingly to those days as Grandpa's "wheeling-and-dealing days."

Returning home that year from school, I noticed a lot of changes. Most of my cousins and friends had started to drink and party all weekend. There was even evidence of family violence and I couldn't accept that people I cared about and respected would hurt each other.

Children were being neglected and subjected to all kinds of "sights and sounds" they shouldn't have been subjected to. When I first saw a man hitting and kicking his wife, I couldn't believe it. When women and children sought protection at my grandparents' home, I grieved and suffered with them.

The houses, which were brand-new the year before, had windows boarded up and some even had pillows stuck in them in an effort to keep out the cold or mosquitoes, depending on the season.

There was no longer any respect for the Mounties. In Cedar Lake, we'd rarely seen them because our reserve constable did an effective job. I had always looked upon the RCMP with a lot of pride.

Now they were only coming to take my people away and lock them up. Even today I still get apprehensive whenever I see an officer, but fortunately we have managed to keep our distance.

There wasn't much respect for parents and elders either. Children were abusing our elders, emotionally and physically, but then this was a two-way street.

I fought against this monster called alcohol, but in later years I was to become a statistic myself. I drank mostly to be a part of the group and because I wanted to portray the kind of person that society perceived me to be. In a way, I guess I felt I could get back at Manitoba Hydro by making them feel guilty for the way we turned out.

I managed to finish high school and even squeezed in one year of university. However, the call of the North got to me and I returned to live in northern Manitoba. I got married and had a son.

Today, when I watch my son play, I often reflect on what could have been. I grieve for the cousins and friends who at very tender ages are now being subjected to the harsh realities of life. I compare their lives to my own growing-up years in Cedar Lake.

My life then was so peaceful, full of contentment and love. I dream of the time my son could have had, fishing in the same lake I did, attending the same church I did, and just enjoying God's gift of life to the fullest. I can appreciate that everything was done in the name of progress, but whose progress?

June of 1989 marked twenty-five years since we moved from Cedar Lake. Some refer to it as celebrating the twenty-fifth anniversary of our move, but for me, June is a time of mourning for what my people lost. Not only their spirit and dignity, but the beautiful, serene land we gave up. When we gave up our land, it seems like we also signed away our birthrights and the futures of our children.

The $104 each of us received from Manitoba Hydro will never come close to alleviating this feeling of betrayal and pain I feel in my heart and soul to this day.

ELLEN GABRIEL

KANESATAKE: THE SUMMER OF 1990

In the summer of 1990, Mohawks living in Kanesatake, Quebec, erected a blockade to prevent the municipality of Oka from expanding a golf course on traditional Mohawk land. A Quebec police officer was killed when the Sûreté du Québec raided the barricade. The raid and shooting sparked a seventy-eight-day armed stand-off.

IT IS DIFFICULT TO KNOW where to begin the story of the so-called Oka Crisis, especially since so many who do not even know the true story have claimed to be able to explain why those events took place. I suppose one could write an epic novel on the subject, but I suspect that will not happen: the truth is hard to swallow for most Canadians.

History in Canadian schools has been taught from a very biased and racist point of view. Native people have much educating to do, both of the public and of themselves, concerning the true history of our culture and our people.

Kanesatake, or Oka, as it is most commonly known, has always been a Kanienkehaka community. Kanienkehaka is our own name for ourselves; it means People of the Flint. To outsiders we are known as Mohawk, one of the five founding nations of the Iroquois Confederacy.

Even before any European set foot on this continent, Kanesatake was flourishing in every sense of the word. Located near the confluence of two major waterways, the Ottawa and St. Lawrence rivers, Kanesatake was a central location for many nations besides the Kanienkehaka people. Pottery shards found at Oka Park date back as far as 1000 BC. Agriculture and the exchange of goods amongst different native nations were taking place long before any white man developed the idea of the fur trade.

When the businessmen-disguised-as-priests of the Sulpician order first arrived in Kanesatake from France, they did so under a land grant from the king of France. However, in Kanienkehaka culture, as in any other Iroquoian cultures, the women are known as the custodians of the land. If any land is to be sold or given to another nation, the process must be overseen by the women of the Iroquois Confederacy. The Canadian and American governments have never been able to produce any documents showing that the women of the Kanienkehaka nation gave, sold or ceded any of our lands to them, or to the French or English who preceded them.

Since the arrival of Europeans in North America, native people have been coerced, killed and maimed to allow non-native culture to prosper. In Kanesatake, my ancestors were jailed for cutting wood to heat their homes and cook their food. If they refused to convert to Roman Catholicism while in jail, they remained there until they died. Many missionaries used Christianity to exploit the native people and to justify their governments' policies of genocide.

When Canada was being formed, the British Parliament passed the British North America Act, a racist act that declares sovereignty over every native nation in Canada. This declaration was meant to override all the treaties made with individual native nations who were supposed to be allies, not servants, of the British monarchy or empire.

The same racist attitude, based on the non-native belief that their way of life, their religion and their system of government are far superior to those of any native nation, still reigns today in the structure and actions of the Department of Indian Affairs and Northern Development (DIAND). DIAND created the band-council system, in which the Minister of Indian Affairs is the grand chief. It does not matter how intelligent or educated a native chief is in the white man's ways; when it comes to the crunch, it is the Minister of Indian Affairs who has the final say in any program affecting native people's lives.

Over the past twenty years, as band-council systems became more predominant and the Indian agent position was phased out, the federal government began working out deals with those people of native descent who had little or no respect for their own traditional forms of government and culture. These people made deals that helped the government perpetuate the genocide that has been going on against native people for almost five hundred years now.

THE BLOCKADE

When we started our blockade of an access road in the Pines on March 9, 1990, we did so because most of us had lost faith in the system which is called "justice." But we had lost faith even more completely in the band-council system. Closed-door meetings and secret agreements between the Feds and the Six Nations Traditional Hereditary Chiefs (the misleading name for the band council in Kanesatake) had led many of us to the conclusion that the only way to stop the illegal development of our land was to take matters into our own hands.

At first, the people who participated in the twenty-four-hour vigil came from different backgrounds. By this I mean those of the Christian faith, atheists, and of course, the Haudonosaunee, or People of the Longhouse, which is truly the traditional political, cultural and religious structure of the Iroquois and includes all the people who still follow the traditional ways.

During the period that led up to the police raid of July 11, those of us who watched over our Pines were harassed by a vigilante group known as Les Citoyens d'Oka, and by the Sûreté du Québec. These events usually took place at night, often when the barricade was being guarded mainly by women.

For example, one night, several men dressed in black came

and tried to take our banner down. When we caught them in the act, they ran away across the golf course, within clear sight of where the SQ patrol cars were parked to keep us under surveillance. Yet the SQ did nothing about the incident.

Other times, usually late at night, members of Les Citoyens d'Oka would drive up the highway to the access road where we had our blockade, stop to shout obscenities at us and give us the finger, then gun their motors and squeal their tires as they spun round and raced away.

On May 1, 1990, a police raid was called off in the final planning stages after we found out about it. Representatives from the federal government and the province met with the People of the Longhouse. On May 2, 1990, a few of our men reported seeing the police harbouring boxes of guns in one of the sheds in the golf course. The police, of course, denied it, and told the press we were trying to hamper negotiations.

The two governments in the meantime offered us nothing new. What we had asked for in order for the blockade to be removed was to have, in writing, a guaranteed moratorium on all development within a 253-square-mile area. No one would give us the guarantee, so the blockade remained.

Over the past year and a half, I have heard many community members point accusing fingers at one another over who brought in the weapons. This issue is irrelevant as far as I am concerned, since it was also irrelevant to the Sûreté du Québec. The police did not care whether the men, women and children at the Pines were armed or unarmed when they opened fire. To say we asked to be shot at is like saying the Jews asked for the Holocaust.

To condemn the Kanienkehaka people who defended the lives of their families against a police force totally out of control, is to condone the human rights abuses commited by the SQ. The governments of Canada and Quebec allowed these abuses to continue, with resulting damage to their reputation as defenders of human rights in the international community.

I realize that the propaganda against the Kanienkehaka people of Kanesatake, Kahnawake, and even Akwesasne, has damaged our credibility in the public eye. However, as far as I am concerned, no one is as immoral as the bureaucrats who wanted to send in the army on July 12, 1990, even at the risk of bloodshed.

Jean Ouellette, the mayor, and Gilles Landreville, the deputy-mayor of the Oka town council played pivotal roles in creating an atmosphere of hysteria among the public by telling the press the Kanienkehaka were threatening the lives of the non-native residents of Oka. Nothing could have been further from the truth. On the other hand, the Oka town council stood to lose millions of dollars in revenue if the golf course expansion did not go through.

As traditional people, we are obliged under our own law, Kaienerakowah, to stop any encroachment upon our land. In spite of a 1924 resolution passed in the Canadian Parliament outlawing the government of the Iroquois Confederacy, we, the Haudonosaunee, still maintain that we are the only legitimate government who can negotiate concerning the lands of our territory. Band councils are only an extension of the Department of Indian Affairs.

Throughout the period that led up to July 11, 1990, the Kanesatake Haudonosaunee reached out to other members of the Confederacy for help and advice about what to do in this situation which has deteriorated continuously over the past two hundred years. All people of every Longhouse were asked to attend a meeting in Kanesatake, and to put their personal differences aside. However, it was only two months earlier that two deaths had occurred in community conflicts at Akwesasne, so we knew that there would be a problem in that direction as far as unity was concerned.

I must also stress that the Kanesatake blockade was never a "Warrior" blockade. Everyone was asked to unite, including the members of the Warrior Society and those who opposed them. The Warriors were allowed to fly their flag, however, just as the Micmacs were. The press took off with the notion that we were all members of the Warrior Society. The Longhouse people in Kanesatake established the initial barricade on the access road, and since we are citizens of the Kanienkehaka nation, this was an issue for all the people of the nation, not just the Warrior Society.

In the meantime, while we were trying to reach all members

of the Iroquois Confederacy, the Municipality of Oka continued in its path of destruction. Jean Ouellette held press conferences to assure his investors that their project would go through in spite of our determination not to vacate the Pines.

On June 23, 1990, in Ottawa, the Haudonosaunee advised the Minister of Indian Affairs, Tom Siddon, that he could not make any deals with the band council, the Six Nations Traditional Hereditary Chiefs (since renamed the Mohawk Council of Kanesatake) concerning the land, since the band council is only an extension of the Department of Indian Affairs and not a legal entity in a position to negotiate lands within Kanienkehaka territory. The traditional government of the Haudonosaunee participated in the original treaties, and they, not the makeshift governments of the band-council system, are the legal entities authorized to negotiate land treaties. Besides, the women of the Haudonosaunee have never signed away the future of children the way the band councils have been doing.

It was at the June 23 meeting that Mr. Siddon told the Haudonosaunee and the band council under Chief George Martin that there was no money left in DIAND's budget to "buy" land for the Kanesatake Kanienkehakas. This is a ridiculous statement to us; how can we buy back something that is already ours? The federal government should compensate the people to whom they fraudulently sold land in the first place — not take it out of Indian Affairs' budget.

We returned to Kanesatake and immediately went back to our vigil in the Pines.

THE POLICE RAID

Some community members, including some of the traditional people, were predicting violence and bloodshed. They even made statements like: "It's not worth dying for." Those of us who did not leave the Pines wondered why these people were making such statements. We did not feel our lives were on the line. We felt the police would come in using excessive violence, possibly beating us, but we never imagined they would actually shoot at us.

On July 10, Mayor Ouellette made a public statement requesting the Sûreté du Québec's assistance in dismantling our barricade. When asked whether he was worried about the possibility of bloodshed, he answered that it was not his concern. He was only asking the SQ to enforce the law against those who were breaking the law.

Reporters asked us at the barricade what we would do if the SQ came in to dismantle the barricade. We replied that we would inform them they were trespassing and that they had no jurisdiction on Mohawk Territory. We expected to be arrested for public disobedience. We never thought they would fire concussion grenades, tear gas and, eventually, aim and fire their M-16s at us.

At approximately 2:00 a.m. on July 11, several members of the community, including Allen Gabriel and the band council, were informed of the SQ raid that was to take place in the Pines at 5:15 a.m. These people, however, never informed those of us sleeping overnight at the Pines that there would be a raid.

What took place on the morning of July 11, 1990, was the attempted perpetration of murder and genocide against an identifiable group of traditional people of the Kanienkehaka Nation. We were and still are a thorn in the side of the illegal government known as Canada. But through our belief in our Creator and our perseverance in our ceremonies, we were spared and have lived to tell about the morning of July 11 and the summer of 1990 in Kanesatake. Some bureaucrats wanted the Canadian army brought in from the start to finish the stand-off. However, politicians like John Ciaccia, the Quebec minister in charge of Indian Affairs, did try in earnest to peacefully end the seige. People like Mr. Ciaccia were in the minority.

I will never forget the summer of 1990, nor will anyone else who lived behind the barricades in Kanesatake and Kahnawake, I imagine.

We did not initiate the violence of 1990, nor do we feel it was our first and only choice, as the government of Canada has led the public to believe.

I believe in survival. My nation, and especially my ancestors, understood the extremes people have to go to in order to protect what is rightfully theirs. We are a peace-loving nation, otherwise hardly any non-natives would have survived the centuries of "European Contact" in North America.

The policy of genocide is unacceptable in the name of God. These days, of course, it is carried on in the guise of enforcing the Indian Act and perpetuating the band councils.

My nation has been fed lies by Tom Siddon and his bureaucrats. DIAND has never compensated the Municipality of Oka for the parcel of land where we were fired on. They bought an adjacent parcel of land, but not the Pines area that was intended for the golf course itself. In fact, the Pines is still slated for development — condominiums — but that project has been put on hold for now too.

Justice in Canada is non-existent at the present time in the story of the "Oka Crisis." The real criminals and terrorists who held guns and canons to Kanienkehaka women, children and men have been rewarded with public accolades from Canadian Prime Minister Brian Mulroney and others. Meanwhile, our people went to trial.

What is apparent to us is that the government of Canada has no intention of honouring our treaties. Instead we continue to struggle with tokenism in the new "Reformed Constitution," although our rights have already been, and still are, entrenched in the treaties, in our own laws and in international law. Unfortunately, Canada respects international law only when it does not apply to itself.

As a Kanienkehaka woman, I would still like to see peace between native people and ordinary Canadians, for I know that the politicians do not represent the people's voice. Until that day, all of us should continue to seek the truth and justice, for what it's worth, in all our environments.

FIGHTING BACK

As traditional legal and political avenues led to dead ends in the aboriginal struggle for justice, some people felt they had no alternative but to take up arms in defence of their rights. Loran Thompson of the Mohawk Nation is one person who has been involved in armed resistance — at both Akwesasne and Kanesatake, Mohawk communities near the Quebec-Ontario border. His opinion is a controversial one, held by only a minority of aboriginal people living in Canada and in the above communities. It needs to be heard and understood, however.

Thompson does not speak for Kanesatake. Very few residents of that community would say they "chose" to take up arms to defend their land. Governments, businesspeople, the courts, the police, the media, and Mohawk and non-Mohawk native people from outside the community also played significant roles in the escalation of events during the summer of 1990. But Thompson was a supporter of the armed resistance at Kanesatake. He also acted as a member of the negotiating team before the siege began. He was one of the people surrounded in the treatment centre in the last days of the siege, and escaped during the ensuing confusion when the Mohawk people decided to end the seige. He went to visit family, then turned himself in to the police several days later. He discusses his experience and his convictions in the following article, based on a conversation with John Bird.

I HAVE BEEN INVOLVED for a long time with my father and mother in the fight for Indian political rights. I have been more directly involved since 1975, when I was appointed one of the representatives of the Bear Clan in the community council at Akwesasne. The community council is sanctioned by the People of the Longhouse and by the Iroquois Confederacy.

In 1979, the New York police and the Indian Police (who enforce both state and federal law) came to my house, which is in the part of Mohawk Nation territory known as Akwesasne and in the part of Akwesasne that is surrounded by what is known as the State of New York. This was after an incident involving trespassing by the members of a conservation crew.

The Longhouse said: "You are not going back to jail; this is a jurisdictional fight."

I said: "I am a servant of the people and I will do whatever the people ask of me, but if I do this, you have to protect my family."

This led to an armed stand-off with State of New York police forces that lasted two years. In the end we proved that neither the state government nor the federal government had jurisdiction and that the police had acted illegally in coming to pick me up.

We didn't start the armed confrontation, but both the police and the tribal council representatives had arms, so the Longhouse took up the same stuff.

We have been taken for suckers long enough. You put up the flag of truce and try to talk peace and they massacre you. But it's never going to happen to us again without us putting up a defence. As a nation we have decided we are going to fight for our rights. Only when others on the opposite side to us have taken out their arms have ours come out. Our rights are not going to be given to us on a silver platter. We have to fight for them.

My stand on our sovereignty and rights has never changed. I

have a clear understanding of what we are supposed to be and what we are supposed to be doing. And if it takes armed confrontation, we have no choice but to do what the other side is doing. If they're talking then we're talking. We are always the defenders, not the aggressors. We are always the ones who want to talk.

If we go back to the events of July 11, 1990, when the Sûreté du Québec opened fire on the people of Kanesatake in an attempt to dismantle the roadblock they had erected in the Pines, who are the people who commited a terrorist act in invading a peaceful nation? Who sent their army into a peaceful nation? We did not have tanks and helicopters and jets. We did not have thirty-millimetre automatic rifles and gas bombs. Quebec and Canada were the terrorists. The Mohawks and their allies, known to most Canadians as warriors, were the protectors of our territory and people.

The word "warrior" has been put upon our people by history. Some of us have been willing to accept it, and to refer to ourselves as Warriors, because it is a word that non-Indian people understand. But it is really a mistranslation. Our word is *Rotiskarekethe*, which means "the people who are burdened with preserving or protecting our peace." *Rotiskarekethe* includes both men and women. We have an understanding that we are a nation of people, and we agree with the covenant in the United Nations that says no one nation is allowed to oppress another. Canada is oppressing the Indian nations in a gross way.

We negotiated right up until the very end, September 26, when we were on our way home. We did not give up and we were not defeated; we just decided to go home. But then we were again attacked by the Sûreté du Québec, and the defence mechanism — the fight or flight response — kicked in, and we did fight back.

Personally, I have never taken up arms in any of these confrontations. I have never picked up a weapon. That has been a strategic decision. In a confrontation of any sort, you always need credible people to negotiate; that's why I have not taken up arms myself. I was with the people you know as Warriors, but I was not their leader. But I do support the defence in any manner, shape or form, of our territory when we are attacked in any manner, shape or form — as any politician in any nation would.

As long as we are willing to deal with land issues on a dollars-and-cents basis, Canada is willing to listen and to sit at the table with us. But when we start talking about our rights to our territory and lands, then Canada is not willing to talk.

Canada has laid out a clear strategy of its own about what it is going to do with its Indian problem. The government keeps putting Indians in a position where they have to fight.

We have never given the right of "eminent domain" (ultimate control of the land, including the right of expropriation) to either Canada or the U.S. We have never said: "You are the supreme authority." In some cases, we have made treaties to allow other people to use the land, but we have never given away the underlying title.

The underlying title to this country does not belong to the Crown, but to the aboriginal people. That's why Canada is not going to sit down and negotiate justly with aboriginal people. They want the Indian people to take up arms and fight.

There are only two ways a government can get title to land. Either it is ceded to them or they have to take it by conquest. We aren't going to cede it, so conquest is their only other option. Our moral code says we have to defend our liberty and our territory for coming generations so they can enjoy what the Creator put here for us to enjoy, not to destroy.

The province of Quebec is going to destroy the James Bay Cree, along with untold amounts of the creation, all in the name of progress, just so we can have as many lights as we want in any room. We are just going backwards. It's all for luxuries. We need to be living a simpler life, so we don't destroy nature.

In defending ourselves, we are also defending nature. We have been here for thousands of years and we have not destroyed creation. Quebec is going to do it in a couple of years.

Every day of our lives is political. Every day, on the highway, dealing with the police, in stores, we are asked: "Are you an Indian? What's your number?"

The siege of Kanesatake in 1990 — and our armed defence of our territory — has mobilized and awakened many Indian people. Kanesatake also showed both the Canadian people and the rest of the world the inability of Canadian politicians to deal with the issue.

Morally, the Canadian people need to push their government into dealing honourably with the Indian people. We have done nothing but deal honourably with governments, but they come back with word games and talk about limited mandates.

Regardless of the differences of opinion among individuals in Kanesatake at the time of the armed forces siege, the majority of people put their differences aside and came together on the issue. Freedom is expensive. Some are willing to go the whole nine yards and some are willing just to talk.

What Canada gives, Canada can take away. That is why we don't want Canada to legislate anything for us — other than to sanction a treaty between the Mohawk Nation and the Canadian government (which we would have to sanction too) as to how we can live side by side in peace.

If there have been any negative results of our armed resistance in Kanesatake, they are minimal. There are a few people within the Iroquois Confederacy who say armed resistance is not the way to go because we have buried our weapons. When the Confederacy was formed before European contact, the five founding nations buried their weapons. But that was only as a sign that there was peace between members, that we would never take up arms *against one another*. We still kept our war chiefs to lead us in defending against invasion.

The chiefs themselves are not allowed to get involved in an armed confrontation because they are supposed to be men of peace. The prime concern of a person who takes the role of the chief is to see peace prevail, and if he cannot do that, then he must turn things over to the men of the nation and the men have to do whatever is in their power to protect our people until peace comes.

I am using the word "chief," but in the Mohawk language, the word is *Roiianer*, and the plural is *Rotiianer*. It means "the ones with the long steps" or "the ones with the far sight." In other words, they are the ones who look deeply into the issues.

There is nothing that Canada can say or do to convince me

that armed resistance is neither necessary nor worthwhile for us. Canada, through its police — its paramilitary — will constantly harass our people and our territories. I believe that our nation, because of history, has to forever stay ready to defend itself because of the mentality of the Canadian politicians and the Canadian police force in attempting to achieve supreme power over our land. Even a mouse has the instinct to protect itself when it is cornered, regardless of how huge its enemy might be.

We knew that Canada would not blow us up when the Canadian Armed Forces had us surrounded at Kanesatake. The Canadian government would not be able to withstand the international response. But even if the Sûreté or the armed forces had done that, we would have been ready to die.

If you are a traditional person aware of your spiritual and political obligations, and you are performing your duties, then you are always prepared to go home — because you are fulfilling the obligations put on your shoulders by your Creator.

The way we prepare is that every morning when the sun comes up, we are grateful to our eldest brother, the sun, whom we call *Rotiskarekethegowa*. When the sun comes up, we give thanks to the sun for giving us energy, power, light and heat. Then we go around and give thanks to all of the natural creation, all the way up to the Creator himself, whom we thank for giving his energies and power. We are thankful that he does not hold them back.

I am at peace with creation and I give thanks to the Creator. I don't ask for the sun to come up, for the trees to grow, for the rain to fall. I am just thankful that they are there and doing their job so we can go about our daily lives happily.

DEAN JACOBS

WALPOLE ISLAND: SUSTAINABLE DEVELOPMENT

OVER A CENTURY AGO a British officer, Major John Richardson, visited Walpole Island and wrote these words about its people:

> As I contemplated this scene and contrasted the really native dignity and simplicity of these interesting people with the loathsome hypocrisy of civilized life, I could not but deeply deplore the fast-approaching extinction as a race of the first lords of this soil, gentlemen of nature whose very memory will soon have passed away, leaving little or no authentic record behind them, of what they once were . . .

These "first lords of the soil," these "gentlemen [and women] of nature" have not passed away. We remain strong and able in our stewardship of our homeland.

The Walpole Island First Nation is an aboriginal community located on the delta joining Lake St. Clair to the St. Clair River. This piece of land is part of the homeland of the Ottawa, Ojibwa

---

This article was adapted from a speech in Windsor, Labour Day, 1990.

and Potawatomi people, who have lived along these waters for thousands of years.

Because of our location, our air, water, wildlife and people have been continually exposed to a wide range of poisons for decades. The water we drink is polluted by toxic emissions from the industries of Chemical Valley centred around Sarnia, from run-offs of pesticides and fertilizers from mechanized agriculture in the region, from municipal sewage discharged from the American shore and from accidental spills from ocean-going freighters and pleasure craft. The air we breathe is contaminated by emissions from the world's largest incinerator located in Detroit and from industrial pollution from America's "Rust Belt."

These are not the only environmental problems we face. Sediments lying on the bed of our delta need to be dredged every two to three years to ensure safe shipping. These sediments hold many poisons that are re-suspended in our waters during dredging and dumping into open waters of Lake St. Clair.

But our people face more than strictly environmental problems. Unemployment is very high at 60 percent. There is little economic diversification in our community because of restrictions imposed by the Indian Act. And we are not able to reap the benefits of many of our natural resources until agreement is reached with the federal and provincial governments on our territorial boundaries. Social and cultural problems common to underdeveloped communities across Canada — be they native or non-native — are also found on Walpole Island.

But not all is gloom. We are endowed with a unique ecosystem of wetlands, Carolinian forests and prairie grasslands. We are rich in fish and wildlife. We have a strong cultural heritage that is celebrated by our people. And we have a community that has the strength and vision to confront its development problems in a way that ensures our continued stewardship of the homeland given to us by our Creator generations ago. Some recent initiatives of the Walpole Island First Nation demonstrate this strength and vision.

Incredibly, there has never been agreement between our government, the federal government and the Ontario government on the boundaries of our territory. In 1989 we signed an historic framework agreement with the other two governments to commence negotiations that will define our territory in the Canadian part of Lake St. Clair and the powers that we will exercise within our jurisdiction either alone or in co-operative agreements with the other governments. For six months these negotiations proceeded smoothly until the federal government demonstrated bad faith through an assault on our natural environment and our people. Without advising us, the federal government began dredging sediments from Seaway Channel.

Walpole Island has always supported the principle of safe shipping. This requires periodic dredging. In the past we had made sites available on our territory for the safe containment of dredged sediments.

On this occasion the federal government maintained that its preliminary environmental impact assessment had shown there were no contaminants. We demanded to see the results of this assessment and were shocked to find that tests for two highly toxic chemicals had not been conducted. Federal scientists working on the Upper Great Lakes Connecting Channels Study (UGLCCS) had identified a potential danger of these toxics being in our sediments but the government did not pay attention to its experts.

The Walpole Island First Nation immediately demanded a stop to the dredging until proper testing was done. The federal government refused. Walpole Island then sued the Ministers of Environment, Public Works and Indian Affairs, and applied for an immediate injunction in the Federal Court of Canada to have the dredging halted.

The support we received from the Windsor community in the dredging scandal was greatly appreciated. They signed our Parliamentary petition and alerted others to our plight. We did not get the injunction, but the Federal Court judge ruled that we had a strong enough case for it to continue to trial.

Testing by Environment Canada the day after the injunction hearing showed that the two toxins we were afraid of were in fact present in the sediments, confirming our worst fears. Walpole Island made several attempts to have its concerns over future dredging addressed in an out-of-court settlement, but federal bureaucrats always countered with watered-down versions that were unacceptable to us.

Finally, in 1991, we reached an out-of-court settlement. Our actions were vindicated and a mutual process was established to prevent future incidents.

SUSTAINABLE DEVELOPMENT

Walpole Island is not a closed community. We live in an ecosystem that knows no political boundary. We have always tried to work with other governments and agencies in addressing environmental problems and development opportunities.

Walpole Island has the majority of the wetlands in Lake St. Clair. We have been pushing for several years to have them designated as wetlands of international importance under the RAMSAR Convention for the Conservation of Wetlands of International Importance as Waterfowl Habitat.

But perhaps the most important initiative we have taken on in terms of the environment and development is our recent move to prepare a strategy for Walpole Island's sustainable development well into the next century.

What do we, as aboriginal people, mean by "sustainable development"? We do not believe that it represents only economic progress in balance with the natural environment. We define sustainable development as equitable social, economic, cultural and technological betterment in a way that does not pollute our ecosystem and deplete natural resources.

Two things should be emphasized in this definition. First, *equity* is the key to sustainable development. For Walpole Island this means that we are no longer willing to sit on the sidelines of progress in this country. We want the shackles taken off so that we can work towards our own economic development.

Secondly, our definition of sustainable development goes beyond economic and technological progress. Sustainable development means the improvement of human resources, improving the capabilities of communities to work toward social, economic, cultural and technological betterment. It depends a lot on having sufficient capital and information resources as well. Simply addressing the proper management of natural resources without paying equal attention to the strengthening of human, capital and information resources will not in the end lead to sustainable development.

It will probably take about a year and a half to prepare our sustainable development strategy. It will come from our community through a process of consensus. We will thoroughly analyze our environmental and development problems and opportunities and then establish as a community our goals and objectives for sustainable development. We will look at various policy options and select the one that best meets our goals. And we will examine institutional changes that are required on Walpole Island and externally in order that sustainable development can occur.

Because we believe in strong coalitions for sustainable development, we plan to consult with a wide range of external role players in preparing our sustainable development strategy. The support we received in Windsor during the dredging crisis shows that others also believe in strong coalitions.

Four kinds of coalitions are needed: among communities in this ecosystem; among special interest groups; among governments; and among First Nations.

Coalitions of communities are needed because we all share this ecosystem. The contaminated sediments dredged and dumped into our waters last fall polluted not only our water but the water of the wider community. The toxics that biomagnify and bioaccumulate in the food chain will have the same effect on everyone's health. The mercury being pumped into the air by the Detroit incinerator is breathed by every community in the region. A strong co-ordinated voice on sustainable development issues is essential if we are to fulfil our responsibilities to all of our children.

Coalitions of special interest groups are also important. Sustainable development cannot be pursued through single interests. In fact, single interests are the reason that we are all in our present crisis. However, special interest groups — and by this I mean labour, environmental organizations and development groups — all have unique experience and expertise which should be shared. Our Heritage Centre, for example, knows more about our wetlands than any other group in the region. We are willing to share this knowledge with others. If Walpole Island is to succeed in its various environmental and development initiatives, we will need to forge new coalitions and strengthen existing ones with special interest groups.

Coalitions among governments are also crucial to sustainable development, and coalitions of First Nations are needed as well. As a people we have become second-class citizens of this country. We have had our lands and resources taken from us. We have had shackles placed on us by federal and provincial governments for generations. Our rights have been trampled.

As we have shown on Walpole Island, with strength and vision, positive change can come from a variety of actions: court cases, negotiations, consultations and communication. We welcome coalitions for sustainable development that recognize our distinct interests, rights and responsibilities as First Nations and stewards of our homelands.

Such coalitions must be based not on sympathy for the plight of aboriginal peoples throughout Canada but on a full understanding of the important issues that First Nations face across this country.

We look forward to continued dialogues with our neighbours as we prepare our strategy for sustainable development.

PRINCIPLES FOR SUSTAINABLE DEVELOPMENT

In an attempt to codify an ethic of sustainable development, Nin.da.waab.jig, the Walpole Island Heritage Centre has prepared the following guiding principles of sustainable development for review and discussion within the community.

1. Sustainable development is not an option: sustainable development is imperative.
2. Resources, and products of these resources, must be distributed equitably.
3. Non-renewable resources must be conserved.

4. Use of non-renewable resources must be substituted with those that are renewable.
5. Renewable resources must be rehabilitated.
6. Resources, the fruits of these resources, and waste caused by their use must be recycled.
7. Non-recyclable waste must be managed to prevent damage to the environment, including human beings.
8. Technology must be positively enjoined in the pursuit of sustainable development.
9. Institutional mechanisms in support of sustainable development must be fair, efficient and based on co-operation.

N IN . DA . WAAB . JIG , W ALPOLE I SLAND
H ERITAGE C ENTRE

W ALPOLE I SLAND IN
2005: A V IEW FROM
THE F UTURE

What would happen if hopes for sustainable development were realized over the next few decades? In the following article written from the viewpoint of the turn of the twenty-first century, Walpole Island "looks back" at how sustainable development was made possible during the 1990s.

R APID ECONOMIC, TECHNOLOGICAL, political, social and cultural changes occurred during the 1990s which successfully set Walpole Island on a sustainable development path reflecting the needs and aspirations of community members. Most of these changes occurred through often difficult negotiations with the federal and provincial governments.

The greatest obstacle to achieving sustainable development on Walpole Island had been for the most part the institutional

Adapted from *A Future of Sustainable Development: Walpole Island First Nation*, Discussion Paper published in April 1990.

mechanisms inflicted on this First Nation since the imposition of the Indian Act in 1876. In the late 1980s and early 1990s, the community undertook a broad and frequently radical series of institutional changes to remove constraints on its sustainable development.

SUSTAINABLE DEVELOPMENT STRATEGY

The first major change was a comprehensive, community-based effort to clearly define goals and objectives for development by the year 2000. A "Sustainable Development Strategy and Implementation Plan" was formulated, one that rested on the unique natural and cultural heritage of Walpole Island. The first step in formulating this strategy was the preparation of a ground-breaking set of "Principles for Sustainable Development"[1] prepared through community consensus in 1990.

Developing the strategy was a difficult task for the community, as it required a collective commitment to rediscovering and articulating traditional environmental ethics and knowledge and the selection of those aspects deemed most appropriate for a sustainable future. The community was therefore engaged in a process of reconstructing the past by re-examining the historical record and collecting oral histories from elders in the community.

The Sustainable Development Strategy that was subsequently prepared took a holistic view of Walpole Island's environment, its socio-cultural aspirations and its prospects for economic development. Although it focused on the First Nation's territory, it recognized that decisions made on much larger spatial scales were having profound effects on Walpole Island's environment and its prospects for economic, technological, social and cultural development.

The strategy broke new ground. It compelled the federal and provincial governments to confront their willingness to translate empty sustainable development rhetoric into concrete financial and jurisdictional commitments. Walpole Island brought pressures to bear on industry and surrounding municipalities on both sides of the border to engage in a process of dialogue and consensus building, key elements on which the success of the strategy was to depend.

Boundaries Settled (Co-management of Resources). Concurrent with the preparation of the Sustainable Development Strategy, Walpole Island in the early 1990s completed tripartite boundary negotiations with the federal and provincial governments. Boundary lines demanded by the First Nation in the late 1980s were eventually accepted by other parties. This historic negotiation served to clearly define the spatial territory of Walpole Island as all of the Canadian side of Lake St. Clair. Recognizing the economic interests of the federal and provincial governments in this region — particularly with regard to such activities as resource management, environmental monitoring, shipping and dredging — the negotiations included an agreement for the co-management of such activities.

St. Clair River Remedial Action Plan. During the 1990s, the St. Clair River Remedial Action Plan (RAP) was completed and accepted by the International Joint Commission.[2] Walpole Island had participated actively in the RAP process through its presence on the Bi-National Public Advisory Council (BPAC)[3] consisting of representatives from involved Canadian and American communities, industry and special interest groups.

Among other initiatives, the RAP proposed a wide range of corrective measures including (1) much more effective monitoring of water quality and sediments; (2) reduction of point-source pollution by 75 percent in the year 2000 and its elimination by 2010; (3) reduction of fertilizer and pesticide use by 50 percent by the year 2000 on agricultural lands surrounding the river, including Walpole Island's Tahgahoning Farm; (4) stringent controls on the speed and type of shipping traffic along the riverway; and (5) mandatory dumping of dredged sediments in environmentally secure containment sites. The latter resulted in the expansion of Walpole's Seaway Island as the preferred containment site and served to stimulate the development of Walpole Island's own commercial dredging opportunities through the acquisition of skiffs, barges and training from the Canadian Coast Guard.

St. Clair Sustainable Development Commission. In the course of its tripartite boundary negotiations, it became clear to Walpole Island that an integrated regulatory mechanism was required to ensure that the First Nation had a voice in developmental and environmental actions occurring beyond its boundaries. Walpole Island initiated the call for a formal Commission in 1990. Its formation comprised the most contentious part of the St. Clair River RAP, as it was perceived by some municipalities to detract from their jurisdictions. In the end, a regime of mandatory communication and consultation on development and environment initiatives was agreed upon, with enforcement left to respective provincial, state and federal governments.

The Commission has proven to be an extremely important vehicle for Walpole Island. It enabled the First Nation to mount concerted and successful opposition to the expansion of Chemical Valley, as called for in the Lambton County Official Plan. It also served to force, through public pressure by citizens' groups, Michigan municipalities to significantly upgrade their sewage treatment plants. Furthermore, it was the vehicle that ensured that all dredged sediments on both sides of the border and of any quantity, however small, were stored and monitored in an acceptable manner.

International Support. Walpole Island's emerging clout in the sustainable development arena was further enhanced on the international scene through the designation, in 1993, of the territory as a "Wetland of International Importance" by the International Union for Conservation of Nature and Natural Resources (IUCN). This international designation provided Walpole Island with a strong basis to argue its ecological uniqueness and the need for careful conservation and pollution control measures in various forums, including the St. Clair Sustainable Development Commission. It also facilitated the obtaining of research and development grants to Walpole Island from international agencies such as the United Nations Environment Program (UNEP) and the IUCN.

Environment Research. By the mid-1990s, the Walpole Island First Nation had attained significant regional, national and international respect as an important and credible aboriginal voice on sustainable development. A proposal made in 1990 to have Walpole Island designated by the International Joint Commission as an "Integrated Environmental Monitoring Site" was finally adopted with the signing of a protocol to the Great Lakes Water Quality Agreement in a ceremony on Walpole Island in 1993. The establishment of research stations monitoring water and air quality, sediments, wildlife, fish and human health served not only to enhance systematic environmental monitoring but also to strengthen the community's technical, scientific and management capabilities through comprehensive training of band members by scientists from the Canada Centre for Inland Waters, who co-managed the project in its early years.

FROM "MANAGEMENT" TO "SELF-GOVERNMENT"

In spite of all these institutional changes, Walpole Island still did not have the sovereign powers required to adequately direct and control its sustainable development. Even though the federal and provincial recognition of aboriginal rights had been entrenched in section 35 of the Constitution Act 1982, these rights remained undefined until the late 1990s, following a long and laborious process of negotiation.

During the 1990s, Walpole Island sought to increase its powers in the context of an existing federal policy (initiated in 1989), which was promoting the implementation of "self-government" negotiations with individual bands. Walpole Island recognized, however, that in reality, this policy focused on First Nation Management, not First Nation Governance or "self-government." Regardless, the band, upon absorbing all the rights it could from the existing Indian Act, entered into tripartite First Nations Management negotiations in 1991. These negotiations eventually resulted in the passing of enabling legislation in Parliament that gave Walpole Island most of the legal, managerial and financial powers that it need to implement its Sustainable Development Strategy.

In the late 1990s, first ministers of all three governments (federal, provincial and aboriginal) finally defined in the Constitution the sovereignty of First Nations. True "governance," as opposed to "management," had finally come to Walpole Island.

Holistic Approach. The community responded quickly to take full advantage of its new status. It instigated the first major test of the federal and provincial governments' resolve on First Nation Governance when it requested, and after five years of negotiations achieved, full membership (along with the Akwesasne First Nation) in the International Joint Commission. Walpole Island quickly assumed its place on the Science Advisory Board and Water Quality Board.

Within a year, it had succeeded in broadening the latter into the Sustainable Development Board, with a much wider mandate that conformed to the First Nation's holistic approach. Walpole Island was finally in the position to push for many of the off-territory provisions of its Sustainable Development Strategy, which had been periodically reviewed and updated by the community.

ECONOMIC DEVELOPMENT

In the early part of the twenty-first century, the Walpole Island First Nation has, through these institutional changes, successfully implemented five major thrusts called for in the Sustainable Development Strategy: wildlife harvesting, agriculture, tourism, science and civil works.

Wildlife Harvesting. Sustainable trapping, hunting and fishing remain important traditional economic pursuits at Walpole Island. Band members are now engaging in these activities on wetlands that have been expanded by 10 percent since 1990. It was recognized that better monitoring and control of the activities of non-native sports hunters and fishermen was necessary to preserve the integrity of the wetlands and adjacent waters.

Consequently, indigenous training programs for community members to serve as guides were developed while the traditional stewardship role assigned to certain elders in the community was rekindled. Aquaculture was also successfully implemented and the stocking of sports fish and the development of freshwater shrimp farming was made feasible by drastic reductions in point and non-point source pollution upstream and by higher temperatures caused by global warming.

Agriculture. Agriculture was restructured so as to reduce corn and soya bean production at the Tahgahoning Band Farm to 50 percent again due, in part, to higher ambient temperatures. An extremely lucrative organic farming operation which supplies vegetables and fruits to southern Ontario and Detroit area markets was instigated. It served to enhance the nutritional standards of the Walpole Island residents while setting a precedent for similar ventures in the surrounding farming communities. Other new developments included an expanded grain-drying operation to service surrounding farms and the successful harvesting of wildflower seeds for distribution to hobby gardeners and botanists across North America.

Tourism. Tourism development, while it continued to focus on duck hunting and sports fishing, was greatly expanded through the identification of new "market groups" and the enhancement of existing natural and heritage resources. The construction of interpretation centres, boardwalks and trails in the wetlands, prairie grass stands and the Carolinian forests, effectively attracted naturalists and environmentalists from many parts of the globe. The designation of Walpole Island as a "Wetland of International Importance" greatly assisted such efforts.

A new focus was also placed on co-operative relationships with historians and archaeologists through the completion of four major archaeological digs on the territory and the provision of interpretation centres for the general public.

Vacationing tourists were also targeted as a potential market. Controlled recreational opportunities were developed — the beaches are now safe for swimming and dredged sediments are safely contained; Seaway Island now functions as an active recreational area with campgrounds and beaches operated by Walpole Island; and a marina has been built near the ferry, hosting several arts and crafts shops, restaurants, and an information centre.

Science. Walpole Island also became the site for a Sustainable Development Research Centre, established as an offshoot of the Integrated Environmental Monitoring Site. The community provides labs and testing facilities to scientists from across North America and it now has its own scientific team in place. The Centre is actively involved in presenting workshops and conferences on sustainable development and publishes a monthly journal with international distribution.

Civil Works. Finally, Walpole Island has taken an active role in directing the development of several civil works projects. A strong indigenous building construction industry has resulted, responding to the housing needs of a significantly increased population which occurred as a result of native out-migration from such centres as Sarnia, Wallaceburg and Detroit and the reinstatement of native women who had lost their status as a result of "marrying out." [4]

Walpole has also set up its own dredging company, which, because of its proximity to dredging sites, has consistently been successful in bidding contracts in the Lake Huron, St. Clair, Detroit River and Lake Erie areas. An indigenous civil contracting company is also established for the purpose of shoreline construction and erosion control.

TECHNOLOGICAL DEVELOPMENT

Walpole Island has implemented some technological developments that have greatly enhanced the sustainability of the territory's environment. A pipeline, first discussed in the 1970s, has been built between Walpole Island, Wallaceburg and Lake

Huron, ensuring a safe supply of drinking water that would not be affected by accidental spills on the St. Clair River or from the latent effects of groundwater contamination. Housing is now concentrated along the main road, and a sewer system has replaced septic tanks. The garbage dump which was leaching into the canals and wetlands has been relocated and contained. Bio-gas has become the principal domestic fuel. Finally, an emergency response plan has been established on Walpole Island, one that is co-ordinated with surrounding communities, the Coast Guard and Environment Canada.

SOCIAL DEVELOPMENT

Several significant improvements have taken place with regard to the social well-being of Walpole Island's residents, particularly in the spheres of health, family services, education and the status of women.

Health. The general health of the community has improved considerably, due in part to the availability of safe drinking water and a wide range of locally produced (organic) food crops. However, some improvements have resulted from reforms in institutional health care.

Public health education programs dealing with such issues as proper nutrition, traditional herbal medicine, family planning, traditional local midwifery and infant child care have been developed and implemented by members of the community. Drug and alcohol rehabilitation and prevention programs that emphasize the importance of community support networks and peer counselling, and which draw heavily on traditional spiritual values, have had considerable success as well.

Education. In 1990, Walpole Island assumed control of its education system, establishing its own school board, which set the curriculum and administered the community's elementary school. A high school was built in 1995. Both schools are currently staffed by indigenous teachers and provide students with the opportunity to learn their native languages and to develop, along with the teachers, programs of study that combine traditional knowledge and values — deeply rooted in the natural environment — with contemporary fields of inquiry. Students are encouraged to participate in a cultural exchange program with other aboriginal communities in Canada, and a scholarship fund has been established for students seeking admission to post-secondary institutions. Student attrition has been reduced to 5 percent, while 75 percent of high school graduates are enrolled in post-secondary education and training. Finally, the community has produced an impressive core of managers, administrators, researchers and technicians.

CULTURAL DEVELOPMENT

By 2005, the Walpole Island Cultural Society, in co-operation with the Heritage Centre, had established a performing and visual arts facility containing studio and rehearsal spaces and a fully equipped auditorium suitable for staging theatre, dance and musical performances by local arts groups and individuals, as well as aboriginal touring companies. Nin.da.waab.jig is at present organizing a series of Writers' Workshops which will provide young local writers with an opportunity to develop their talents and share their insights. Future plans include an annual short story and poetry writing contest and the publication of a monthly writers' magazine. In 1995, Walpole Island organized its first annual summer Festival of the Spirits, which presents the best of artistic endeavour the community has to offer, as well as the "imported" talents of aboriginal groups outside the community and Canada.

EPILOGUE

Community commitment to the ideal of "sustainable development" was galvanized to a large degree by Walpole Island's efforts to pursue First Nation Governance. Walpole Island set an important precedent for other aboriginal communities across Canada engaged in similar struggles. It also demonstrated to the rest of Canada the merits of uniting environmental and economic interests in addressing human needs. Deeply held community aspirations were realized through sustainable, holistic development and sensitivity to finely balanced ecosystems.

III

BECOMING PARTNERS: NON-NATIVE CANADIANS IN THE STRUGGLE FOR ABORIGINAL JUSTICE

GARY POTTS

GROWING TOGETHER FROM THE EARTH

I REMEMBER ONCE COMING ACROSS an old white pine that had fallen in the forest. In its decayed roots a young birch and a young black spruce were growing, healthy and strong. The pine was returning to the earth, and two totally different species were growing out of the common earth that was forming. And none was offended in the least by the presence of the others because their own identities were intact.

When you walk in a forest you see many forms of life, all living together. They each have their own integrity and the capability to be different and proud. I believe there is a future for native and non-native people to work together because of the fundamental fact that we share the same future with the land that we live on.

We will never be able — no matter how smart any race of people becomes, no matter how advanced technology becomes — to build another planet like earth or build a covered bridge to another planet so we can start all over again. We need to acknowledge that *the land is the boss*. We just have to accept that there's a great mystery out there and that we can't change

---

This article is based on a conversation with Diane Engelstad.

the forces of nature. The earth grows and we grow from it. We have found camp-sites of our ancestors that are six thousand years old, buried under four feet of earth. The earth grew from trees and bush living their life cycles and returning to earth after they died.

On n'Daki-Menan ("our land"), we now have two or three generations of settlers — non-indigenous people — who have adopted our motherland as their motherland. Some families know no other home in the world, so they call it their homeland. Our problem in working together at this point is that the non-native people who've adopted our homeland as their motherland have a different source of authority than we do. Our source of authority is the land, the natural elements of the land, the four seasons and the watershed systems in our motherland area, covering four thousand square miles. The non-native people's source of authority is the Ministry of Natural Resources. Before that it was the Board of Trade in England or the Board of Trade in France, and then the colonial or neocolonial administrations which eventually became the Ministry of Natural Resources. The laws that come from there have dictated what the settlers can do on their land, on their adopted homelands. That is the fundamental difference between us at this point in time: two different sources of authority.

What needs to take place is the transition of authority, so that all authority comes from the land itself, not from an agency that doesn't live on the land and doesn't live with the results of the decisions it makes for the land. And I think where we can agree is that neocolonial institutions have outlived much of their usefulness. We're not demanding that non-native people learn our language, dress like us and be like us. We're saying we have a fundamental commonality that we need to address. Our commonality is the land and how we're going to use the land for future generations.

People who don't live in the area still have a major role to play by informing themselves of the issues and how the system works, and by talking to the government. The Ontario government justifies its actions by saying it is acting on behalf of the people of Ontario. The fundamental question is: Do citizens living elsewhere in Ontario have the right to dictate what the people living on n'Daki-Menan can and cannot do on the land? Ontario citizens have to make a decision. Is the Ontario government, under pressure from industrial and consumer interests in Toronto, the only one that can protect our interests in the area? Or would stewardship be handled better by the indigenous people, the local people?

That's a question well-meaning supporters and environmentalists will have to answer as well. They need to determine in their own minds whether they really believe that indigenous people are capable of making decisions to ensure that the land is kept healthy for future generations. If they feel that we are not capable or if they do not know whether we're capable, then they need to come and talk to us. They need to look at the work we're doing and what our vision for the future is and how it's going to work, and then form their own conclusions based on firsthand knowledge. That's the fundamental systemic problem that we find we have to cope with and tolerate in people. We have been told since the first missionaries arrived that we're not quite human and don't know what we're doing. Even many well-meaning environmentalists inherently believe they are superior to us. For a lot of people, to be superior to an Indian all you have to be is *not* an Indian. And that's a message we don't like to hear anymore.

If people have concluded that we *are* capable, then the practical step is to send letters to the premier supporting our initiatives, asking the government to give those initiatives a chance and to publish regular reports on how they are working.

If the actions are based on understanding, you have the beginnings of a cross-cultural dialogue. In some areas there are wide gaps between cultures, but in some areas the differences are not great.

In a spirit of understanding, we will find ways to grow together from the earth, like the birch and the spruce trees.

ETHEL FUHR

THOUGHTS AND REFLECTIONS

ABOUT TEN YEARS AGO, I was attending a Lutheran convention where Gordon Peters, regional Chief of Ontario, had been asked to conduct one of the forums. He was heckled by two men and finally lost his temper. The following morning the opening plenary exercises were interrupted by a request from Mr. Peters to speak. He apologized for the day before, as losing his temper did not solve anything. The more I thought about it, the more I respected the teachings that produced that kind of man. I wanted to learn more.

Being involved in the social ministries committee of my church, I began to find opportunities to learn about Indian culture and social justice issues. In time I found myself on the national interchurch committee, then called Project North. But my more formative association with Indian people has been right in my local community, working side by side with the Chippewas of Nawash at Cape Croker.

We work together, we plan educational programs for schools together, we work on issues together, we stand at blockades together. Always I come out the winner. I have grown from being with them and seeing their dedication and humour. I have developed a deep respect for their culture and its spirituality. My own spirituality and Christian life has deepened through listening and loving with my native friends. I have come to better understand the command from God, the Creator, to use and care for all of creation so it can be passed on to future generations.

I have learned that all creation is sacred. I cherish my memory of a walk in aid of land claims that I took part in a few years ago. We met at 6:00 a.m. for breakfast and prayers around a fire in an open field. Breakfast was scones and strawberry drink — gifts from Mother Earth. One of the participants that day was an old man who was paralyzed on one side from a stroke. He used a cane and dragged one leg when he walked, or leaned on a car for support. The old man wore a suit and tie for the occasion. When his turn came to say a prayer, he prayed for the life and well-being of his grandchildren. That was why he was there. He travelled along with the walk in a bus that carried not only refreshments for the walkers, but also some of those young children and babies for whose future we were walking.

As we work side by side, it angers me to see the racism in our society. In our favoured "white" society, we have plenty of criminals, "drunkards" and "lazy bums," but we do not label the whole race with those terms. Yet these labels are often used for Indians as a group.

My association with the Indian people has taught me respect for the whole person, not just what's on the outside. Recently, when I was finally able to get a new pair of glasses after major eye surgery, my friends and family complimented me on the "new look." On leaving a meeting with one of my Indian co-workers, I remarked, "You never said anything about my new glasses." Her reply was, "I don't see your glasses, I only see your eyes." What could be more beautiful!

My experience working with Indian people has convinced me that they do not need non-native people speaking for them or telling them what to do. There has been more than enough of that already! Rather, we need to stand with them as they promote what they believe is right for their people, even when it may sometimes be different than what we would do for ourselves. We need to let them know we support them.

JOHN OLTHUIS

STEWARDSHIP AND SOLIDARITY

I BECAME INVOLVED in aboriginal issues in the mid-seventies as Research Director for the Committee for Justice and Liberty, now called Citizens for Public Justice. At the time, we were focusing on the notion of "stewardship" and the need for Canadians to adopt a more responsible lifestyle with respect to the earth's resources.

The stewardship framework brought us face to face with a proposed pipeline that was to carry natural gas along the Mackenzie Valley, right through the land of the Dene people, to southern markets. We were outraged that the government would cater to the wishes of corporations and wasteful consumers, with such a flagrant disregard for the aboriginal rights of the Dene, and for the severe social and environmental impact a pipeline would have. To that end, we participated in efforts to prevent the pipeline from being built.

The pipeline was never built for a combination of reasons — Dene opposition, supported by solidarity coalitions across the country; the recommendations of Justice Thomas Berger, who led a public inquiry; and the fact that the American gas market weakened significantly within a few years.

My starting point for the pipeline issue was a commitment to the principle of stewardship — but the concrete implications became very real as I met the people who had the most at stake. I learned that the Dene struggle was much bigger than whether or not the pipeline would be built; the question was whether they would have control over their way of life and their homeland, as they had had for countless generations.

Georges Erasmus, then president of the Dene Nation, told me at the time that working in solidarity with the Dene meant working to change the structures in my own society. He explained that the Dene people knew what they wanted and how to get there. But what stood in their way and prevented them from being who they truly were, he said, were non-aboriginal values and structures. Georges' words have stuck with me through the decade and a half since, which has been a continuous learning process for me to define my own "solidarity" role. Several years ago, I decided it was time to make a shift away from the more reflective orientation of Citizens for Public Justice and put my principles of justice and stewardship to more concrete use. I began practising aboriginal law and now work with First Nations in many parts of Canada, with involvement in a range of issues from claims and self-government negotiation to environmental hearings on proposed development projects and constitutional recognition of aboriginal rights.

I find that a social justice framework is essential to deal with concrete issues. My personal faith and understanding of the relationship between faith and practice has deepened and grown as I have come to understand more deeply the central place of spirituality in the native struggle for justice and integrity.

Working to change the structures and policies of non-aboriginal society and government is the most difficult but also the most effective way for non-aboriginal people to stand in solidarity with aboriginal people.

RENÉ FUMOLEAU

"ARE YOU WILLING TO LISTEN?"

WHEN I WAS ORDAINED a priest in France in July 1952, I asked
the superior general of my congregation, the Oblates of Mary
Immaculate, to be sent to northern Canada. Fortunately he
accepted. I arrived in Denendeh in Spring 1953, and was sent to
Radeli Ko (Fort Good Hope), then a community of 250 Dene on
the bank of the mighty Dehcho (Mackenzie) River, at the Arctic
Circle.

The seminary and the scholasticate had prepared me little to
live with the Dene, or to understand their situation. The seminary, with its adult male population, had isolated me from older
people and from children, from wisdom and laughter, and I had
not learned to deal with groups who love life more than effi-
ciency. Arriving in Radeli Ko, I didn't know a word of English or
of the Dene language, which didn't appear to be a real problem
for me, as in those days the prayers of the Mass were in Latin.
Regarding relations between different races and cultures, I had
learned only the French colonial experience.

"You the priests and the sisters, you are lucky; you are sure of
going to Heaven," many Dene told me. It seemed that once you
were a priest you had reached the very top. The priest controlled
the Sacraments, and consequently he could control part of the

people's lives. I remember how easy it was for a priest to be very authoritarian.

Recently I visited Radeli Ko. Recalling the "old days" with a few Dene, I asked, "Do you remember what I did or said a long time ago, on such a day or in such a situation?" "Oh, yes," they replied. "It must have looked very stupid to you?" "Oh yes," they replied. "Why didn't you tell me then?" "Well, you were young, you had to make your own mistakes, you seemed to be smart enough to learn one day; we had to give you a chance."

In 1960 I was transferred to Deline (Fort Franklin), on the shore of Sahtu (Great Bear Lake), where I remained until 1968. It was an isolated community, sometimes going two months without mail. The Council of Vatican II took place at that time, and I just wondered how two thousand bishops gathered in Rome could help me to be a priest in Fort Franklin. The Council had been over for three years before I realized the Spirit had rushed in through the newly wide-opened windows.

The years 1967, '68 and '69 were years of searching for people in Denendeh. A powerful revival originated with the Dene at all levels — political, cultural, linguistic, spiritual. Their questioning forced many of us in Denendeh to question ourselves, our roles and situations. Some also feared that the Dene, recovering their own spirituality or trying to revive or protect their culture, risked returning to their "pagan" state and forgetting Christianity. Life in this new situation was a challenge, because, while the Church must question each culture, it must also be part of the culture. I had the feeling that the "old days" were over. Was I ministering in a world that did not exist or in structures that were crumbling? What was the Spirit calling us to?

While in Deline I began taking pictures. I gradually realized that using a camera helped me to understand the missionary process in a new light. Whether I photograph a landscape, an activity or a person, I have to start with what exists. I help this reality to become a photograph, return it to the people, and they appreciate anew their land, their lives and themselves.

By good luck or by grace, my bishop sent me to Yellowknife in 1970. The Indian Brotherhood of the Northwest Territories (now the Dene Nation) had just been formed. Ideas, plans and dreams were growing like willows in springtime. Anything was possible. Denendeh was not yet a province, and the Dene had not yet been coerced into the reserve system, as in southern Canada. The Dene, Metis and Inuit could still achieve self-determination and self-government. The North, with a variety of rich cultures and traditions, could establish political structures better than those anywhere else in Canada, and it could exploit its abundant resources for the benefit of all.

I never knew my exact role in the Dene struggle. I participated with them in meetings, workshops, lectures, celebrations and TV and radio interviews across Canada. What a privilege it was! When they asked for research, I did it; when they asked for audio-visual material, I put it together; when they wanted to bounce ideas off me, I tried to be there. We discussed history, philosophy, culture, theology, ethics, politics and spirituality. And every time I got excited about the possible changes and improvements in the church, one of them stopped me: "Wait a minute, René, you cannot do that for us, we'll have to do it ourselves."

Many years ago I was invited to a meeting of some Dene chiefs, councillors and leaders. After sitting in a corner of the meeting room for the first three days, I asked the person who had invited me: "Why did you invite me anyway?" But he only looked at me and walked by. It took me a bit of reflection, but I figured he was telling me something like this:

> You listened to us discussing the future of our nation, trying to shape our destiny and the destiny of our children. We're trying to break off the bonds of oppression and to decolonize ourselves, we're struggling for self-determination. Isn't it a great honour for you to witness what we're doing? Don't you appreciate our work to rebuild our nation? You and the clergy have been talking for so long! Don't you think that we also have something to say? And are you willing to listen to us?

For people who have been misunderstood, mistreated and despised for so long, my simple presence and my interest were the most positive ministries I could provide. Trying to decolonize myself as much as they were trying to decolonize themselves, we were truly preparing the way for the coming of the Kingdom of God.

In 1975 Project North was born, and I collaborated with this interchurch coalition in support of the creative activities of the aboriginal nations. Working with members of the Anglican, Lutheran, Presbyterian, Mennonite, Quaker, United and Reformed churches helped me to appreciate their faith and also my own. Working with women helped me to become a better man. Working with the Dene helped me to discover what it means to be white or French.

Whether the church, or the Dene Nation or I was successful or not is of no importance. What matters is whether we are still what we are called to be. I discovered that the worst temptation for everyone (or for every institution) is similar to the one Jesus suffered in his agony, on his last night on earth: "Am I still willing to be the person I am called to be?"

I had come to Denendeh with the idea of helping poor people, the "Indians." And now their questions and their challenges were educating me! Their problem was not poverty, but unjust economic and political structures. The Dene were struggling for justice and for self-determination, and it was my ministry to support their creative activities. The people were setting the agenda for the churches, not vice versa. Oh yes, for the church constituencies, for the Dene and for their hundreds of supporters across Canada, there were disillusions. In any true relationship, everyone discovers that everyone else is great, but that nobody is perfect.

Whatever the "success" of the Dene struggle, of the church coalitions, and of my own efforts, we could (and I guess we did) all learn an important lesson: white people and aboriginal people, men and women, young and old, rich and poor, clergy and lay people — everyone and all can help each other discover and correct their own faults, particular to their race, culture, sex, age or religious status. More important, all have their particular qualities and talents, and can help each other to build themselves up. More important yet, all can learn to celebrate together a glimpse of God's kingdom.

LORRAINE LAND

BIBLES AND BLOCKADES

ROAD BLOCKADES AND THE BIBLE are two powerful symbols that represent profound influences on my life. The Bible has shaped my perception of the world and symbolizes some of the most important driving forces for me, particularly a search for greater harmony and justice in society. Road blockades, erected as a last resort by native people in my country to protest the injustices against them and their communities, are also important influences for me. The blockades have come to symbolize the way in which God calls me and other non-natives to work out, in just as radical a way, what "love" means for us as citizens confronted with injustice.

I am sure my situation is like that of many non-native people actively working on aboriginal justice issues. The desire to become involved arises when we recognize that our society systematically and structurally leads to injustice and pain for aboriginal people.

Like many people, I joined an ecumenical coalition on aboriginal justice so that I could *do* something about the injustices facing aboriginal people. I became an active participant in the Edmonton Ecumenical Coalition for Aboriginal Justice (ECAJ, formerly known as the Edmonton Interchurch Coalition on the North). It is one of many native justice coalitions functioning across the country.

I realized that in order to understand the injustices, we needed to look beyond native people to the values of dominant Canadian society. It became clear that the attitudes and values of Canadian society conflict with the beliefs and visions of life embraced by aboriginal people in Canada. Examining the differences between those values and resulting actions prompted a profound shift in how I look at life and how I think about my society and my role in it. I have benefited far more personally from my involvement with aboriginal people through this group than I could ever actually contribute.

The coalition relies on native people to define the appropriate action or advocacy activities for promoting aboriginal justice. We try to avoid having non-natives decide the solutions and political actions. Native people define the problems and solutions, and request groups like ours to participate in the actions. Within the past couple of years, many of the native groups we work with began to tell us to devote less energy to political advocacy on their behalf. The real need for our energy, we were told over and over again, was to educate others within our own circles — in our case our churches and social groups — about our responsibilities to native people.

This was a significant shift from a decade earlier when our coalition was engaged in direct political advocacy for the Dene, for instance. At that time, we were told that our energy was needed to push politically for a Dene land claim. Now, however, our native friends ask us to work to educate our own people. Aboriginal nations such as the Dene have the political leadership and ability to effectively seek political changes themselves, and do it better than we ever could as outsiders. So our task became to educate our peers about appropriate non-native responses to the concerns and demands of people such as the Dene.

Responding to native definitions of the problems and solutions was a challenge for our group. It forced us to really try to understand the unique values and views that would shape those definitions. Sometimes non-natives would have defined the problems and solutions differently.

A commitment to responding to native definitions of the

problems and solutions allowed me to learn about native beliefs and values and about perceptions of justice. The lack of respect for native beliefs and aspirations by the more powerful dominant culture — my culture — has led to the structural injustices natives face in Canada.

Working on native issues has given me the opportunity to step out of my culture's ways of thinking, and look back in. When I look at my society and culture in this way, I see values and practices which concern me, puzzle me, and which I sometimes find abhorrent. Having seen my society's values from the "outside," I can more consciously choose the ones with which I concur and reject the ones I oppose.

After travelling in Denendeh (the Dene name for their land), for instance, I had to look critically at the destructive ideas in my society about our relationship to the earth. The Dene understanding of the interrelatedness of all creatures, both animate and inanimate, has challenged my perceptions of the role of human beings on earth. I believe the view I grew up with — that people should dominate creation, rather than live in harmony with it — is fundamentally distorted and has had tragic global consequences.

I have also been challenged by aboriginal friends and acquaintances to look at the important role of communal responsibility in a healthy society. The influence of individualism on my culture, with its emphasis on personal fulfilment, differs dramatically from aboriginal models of community and resource sharing. This contrast has accentuated the pain and brokenness I see in my society, caused by the pervasiveness of individualism and the resulting loss of communal values.

The native groups our coalition works with often question day-to-day assumptions about the way our society works. Native friends and acquaintances have pointed out to me the intrinsic value our society gives to concepts like time and money, for example. We often fail to remember, in mainstream Canadian culture, that things like money and time have no value in and of themselves, but are only as important as the value we assign to them.

In addition to benefiting enormously from the wisdom and

insight of native people while involved in this ecumenical coalition, I also greatly value my contact with the many wonderful non-native colleagues with whom I have worked. Regularly meeting people from a variety of faith backgrounds has deepened my own understanding of things that are of fundamental concern to people of all faiths. All of us in the coalition, despite our diverse religious traditions, share values like the need to work for the dignity and just treatment of all people, especially marginalized groups.

On many occasions, I have heard my Coalition colleagues express the opinion that we are in some ways more comfortable, and feel more affirmed, in our interfaith work than we feel in our worshipping communities. I believe this is not only because of similar interests, concerns and convictions, but also the result of growing together in an understanding of life that reflects our contact with native people.

Direct contact between aboriginal people and non-native people who support the native struggle for justice is crucial to the real success of the support coalitions. Personal relationships between native people and those who support them complement the more abstract and theoretical commitment to aboriginal justice. Aboriginal justice coalitions can maintain their integrity only if they build strong personal links with the people they are supporting.

Occasionally our group had the privilege of hearing a native acquaintance or visitor share his or her personal life story. Stories were extremely important to us, as they helped us understand the value framework for the justice demands of our native brothers and sisters. Personal contact made us face the very real pain and brokenness in our native friends' lives — pain that results from the unjust structures in our society. Any advocacy in which our group engaged, therefore, was based on a commitment to promote healing, in the lives of real people who had shared their stories so generously with us, and in the communities to which they belonged.

As a Christian I am strongly committed to that healing. But I discovered through my involvement with the Edmonton Ecumenical Coalition that my own life, and my society, need tremendous healing in other ways. I am grateful for this insight, and for the healing I have experienced because of what native people have shared with me.

Like many Christians, my life is a continual struggle to find ways to serve God and my fellow human beings. My search for service has been profoundly influenced by my contact with native people and their values. I have been richly blessed through my involvement in the native justice coalition. I can say with sincerity that I have been given far more by native brothers and sisters than I could ever give them in return.

LOIS CAPE

OKA: 1990 AND BEYOND

LIFE IN A WAR ZONE. . . . How to describe it to someone who hasn't had the experience?

We've heard about how it was for people in Germany, France and Belgium during World War II, and we regularly see the effects of revolution in Central America and Africa on TV. But to have your laundry line ripped down by passing tanks, to have razor wire strung across your lawn, to wake up to soldiers lounging on your front porch or even more insulting, setting up their portable "john" in your driveway . . . these were the realities of everyday life in Oka, Quebec, in the summer of 1990.

These were merely the inconveniences, a very few of them. There were even harsher realities, such as forever having to show identification and being subjected to searching in order to go back and forth to your own home. Having guns pointed at the heads of your children as though they were criminals. Never knowing when you left the town on an errand if the authorities would suddenly change the rules and not allow you back home. Never knowing when your sons might not get home because they'd been picked up for "questioning" (anything from intimidation to torture).

This article originally appeared in the October 15, 1990 issue of *Anglican Magazine*.

I grew up here in Oka. I went to school with the Indian kids. Because I arrived at the big Two Mountains school on the bus from Oka, the other kids considered me "one of them dumb Indians" too. But far from complaining, I was proud to stand beside them and help them face the racial prejudice that existed even then. As we grew up, the friendship grew too. I learned beading with the Indian girls, went out with the boys, got to understand the language fairly well at one point. The only place I feel really at home is here in Oka with the people, the land and the pines that are most important to me.

It's a rare privilege to live in a trilingual village and absorb as much as possible of each of the cultures. Although I am Anglican and my church is in Two Mountains fifteen miles away, I feel as much at home in our local Catholic church (French), the United church (English and Mohawk), and I've had the privilege of attending the Mohawk longhouse for weddings and funerals. God, our Creator, is found in all these houses; through different traditions and ceremonies, it's still the same God who reaches out to us and calls us all His people.

So why do I support the Indians? Because I believe their land claims are legitimate. Because I am proud to see them rising up to take their rightful place on this continent as an independent people. Because I want them to get the recognition they deserve as the first people. And because I have the honour to call them my friends.

There was a way around living in a war zone in the summer of 1990, a way to avoid the inconveniences and even make a buck in the process. You could leave your home and friends behind to take their chances while you lived high on the hog in a luxury hotel, a nice vacation at the expense of the provincial government. Then afterwards you could apply for a fat compensation cheque to cover any damages incurred in your absence, such as tank tracks in the lawn, broken hinges and unfamiliar telephone charges.

This system of running out was called "voluntary evacuation," and it cost the taxpayer a bundle. Many residents accepted this invitation and they mocked those of us who stayed behind. But we had our reasons.

Personally, I could not turn my back on my home and go off to live in another town with only the media to rely on for news. We spent a lot of time with newspeople of all types during the summer. And it became very clear that stories are not always told in the way they actually happen. There are certainly those that are accurate, but there are also those that are exaggerated and those that show a large amount of "artistic licence." What peace of mind would there be in moving away and never knowing what was really happening?

We also felt that those who stayed were playing an important role in keeping an eye on the occupying forces. If we turned tail and ran for our own comfort and convenience, we would have been leaving them a clear field to commit whatever acts of aggression and destruction they were ordered to, without the eyes, ears and cameras of the public on them.

But honesty was really the main factor. How could you live with yourself if you knew you had accepted sell-out money, a government bribe to get out of the way? The governments wanted no witnesses to the final scene of this conflict, but they forgot that not everyone's values are for sale.

We stayed to defend what is ours and to support the people who were defending what is theirs. This land has always been theirs, a traditional summer hunting and fishing ground. Then the Christianized Mohawks moved here with the priests to form a year-round settlement. The land was "granted" to the Indians in perpetuity, in care of the priests. How generous, to give them what was actually theirs!

The Mohawks had a different concept of land ownership and management, and by the time they had caught on to white society's devious ways, the land that was theirs had been largely sold off or granted to others. Squeezed onto a small parcel of their rightful land, they began to struggle to regain what had been lost. But in those days they were uneducated and unused to dealing with white society in legal terms. Even thirty years ago when the original nine-hole golf course was built on land that had been known as the Common and enjoyed by all, they failed in a legal action to prevent the takeover.

But the young leaders of today have the education; they are

familiar with the legal system that supplanted their own; they can hire the best lawyers, and some are lawyers themselves. So with their backs to the wall and their last piece of natural land threatened by golf course expansion and condominiums, they fought fire with fire. Through legal means and negotiations, they attempted to retain this land, which includes their cemetery and their lacrosse field.

The mayor and council were unreceptive, seeing only the almighty dollar at the end of the tunnel, and intended to brush aside the Mohawks and proceed with the work anyway.

But a blockade was set up on the small dirt road that crosses the forest. The mayor was affronted and brought down an injunction to remove this obstacle set up by what he called "armed terrorists" on a "public road" — actually a peaceful protest camp on a bunny trail.

The Mohawks knew that if they were to abandon that position, there would be no second chance. Work on the golf course would proceed in spite of any pending court case, which would be dragged out interminably. They might even have been accorded a Royal Commission, but the end result — in how many years? — would have been a golf course, condos and a report saying, "Gee, that shouldn't have happened! Oops! Sorry!"

So the blockade remained, the mayor called in the Sûreté, and the rest is a proud chapter in North American Indian history.

The peace camp was the most beautiful thing to come out of all this. It started in the provincial park outside the village, at the outer road block. Here you could find people of all races and colours joining their native brothers and sisters in a demonstration for peace and justice. The spiritual ceremonies, the burning of sweetgrass, the tobacco offerings, the prayer meetings, the hymn sings, were all united in the one cause. Each respected the other's customs; all were welcome to pray together.

The focus was on the besieged Warriors, the fight for self-determination and the hope of recognition and respect on behalf of all governments and authorities. The mood was one of total commitment. The sense of peace, power and love felt in that camp was beyond description. Building up that feeling and sending it out to the people inside Kanesatake, to the people in

Quebec and Ottawa, to the people in uniforms in our area, was the *raison d'être* of the camp, the strongest way to help the conflict come to a satisfactory conclusion.

As we stood together at the camp one Sunday morning, we saw an eagle flying overhead, and we all felt it was a sign that our prayers were heard and were carried onward by the wings of our faith.

Although the camp was bounced around from place to place and the people in the camp were harassed by the Sûreté, the army and the park authorities, it continued to thrive until the end when the police shut it down and wiped it out with fire hoses. But our prayers for peace were answered in the sense that no further major battles or deaths had occurred.

In the minds of most Canadians, the show was over on September 26, when the people under siege finally left the treatment centre. The scene on the street that night was far from peaceful, as the army and police were waiting to get revenge on those proud defenders who had dared to hold back the whole country for so long. Again I was present, and so were my children, getting a firsthand lesson in Canadian history as it happened. I wouldn't have wanted it any other way. This was education, the kind you can't get from history books.

In July of 1992, the matter of what to do with the Mohawk Warriors was finally settled by the courts. Two Warriors are in prison, and the thirty-five others have been acquitted of all charges. Many people have praised the jury's decision as a turning point in the court's treatment of aboriginal people. And indeed, it seems to bode well for future relations between aboriginal people and the rest of Canada.

But what of the main question underlying it all: the land? Who knows? One gets the feeling that all that was gained from that summer's conflict is the sympathy, the solidarity, the respect of the Canadian people and a growing awareness on their behalf.

No longer do we lead anonymous lives in a sleepy little town that barely appears on the map and whose chief claim to fame is cheese. We were swept up by the events of the summer of 1990 to become part of history, each doing our part in our own way to bring about the conclusion we believe in. We were raised out of our complacent cocoon to a new awareness of political realities, social injustices and the need to struggle for peace and freedom. We all grew a lot, learning to help in any way we can the great Whole of which we are each a part.

M U R R A Y   A N G U S

NATIVE ISSUES AS A POINT OF ENTRY

*C*ONTRADICTIONS.

That's what gave rise to my first "political" act.

It involved simply asking a question, perhaps the simplest question of all: *Why?*

Asking "why?" is always a *political* act, because it means not accepting the *status quo* without question.

In my case, I questioned the position of aboriginal people in the world around me. My direct experience of aboriginal people contradicted what I was being taught about them by the dominant society I was part of.

Much of what we come to "know" about the world comes first from what other people tell us about it. First we learn from family and friends, and later from teachers, members of the community and the media. Only later as we grow do we actually learn directly about the world from our own experience. As we listen to others tell us about the world, we absorb not only facts, but values, judgements, biases and prejudices about people.

In most cases, I believe, our own interpretation of the world ends up conforming with what we have always been taught . . . unless our own experience proves to be so powerful and persuasive that it's impossible to deny its validity. . . .

As a teenager growing up on the outskirts of Thunder Bay, I stood between two worlds. As a white Anglo-Saxon male, I had more than my share of connections with the dominant culture in the city. At the same time, as a poor kid living in a cabin beside the reserve, I had a basis for feeling close to the people who were my neighbours.

Indians were a part of my life from the beginning, and it was probably that which made me particularly attuned to the "messages" I was receiving about them from the white community. If I could sum up that message, it would be this: "Indians are at the bottom of the social ladder — *and that's where they deserve to be.*" Contained in this "message" were two things: a description (of their socio-economic status), and a judgement (on their worth as human beings). Innumerable reasons would be given to uphold and reinforce these viewpoints, of course, and they would be expressed in subtle and not-so-subtle ways at both a public and a private level. All of this added up to make the message one of the clearest, loudest, most consistent and pervasive ones that emanated from the white community when I was a kid.

Had I, like most people in the city, never had any personal contact with people from the reserve, I would probably never have had any reason to doubt the accuracy of this message. Indeed, like most, I would probably have contributed — knowingly and unknowingly — to its reinforcement, and thus helped to pass it on to succeeding generations.

But my circumstances were different. I had a lot of contact with people on the reserve. They were my neighbours and friends. We played together, fought together, laughed together, spent endless summer days in the bush together. Our parents worked together, and in turn, so did we. I may have been white, but I felt familiar with, and welcomed in, *their* community.

And that's what my experience was: of people who were warm and welcoming, who outwardly lacked a great many of the material things that so preoccupied white society, but who were nonetheless able to enjoy life with a tremendous amount of humour, openness and generosity towards others. As I moved back and forth between the two communities, it became very clear to me that there were certain qualities to reserve life that could not be matched by anything in the white community. I began to feel privileged that I had not only the chance to experience it, but to be enriched by it.

As my appreciation for the native community grew, so did my awareness of the contradictions between my own experience and everything I had previously been taught about Indians. My experience was telling me — with great clarity and conviction — that Indians had something that was both different and very valuable to share with the larger society. The message that continued to come from the white community, however, was that Indians had nothing of value to offer, and that their lowly socio-economic status was an accurate reflection of their value as human beings. As the gulf between the two grew, I had to choose which I was going to trust more.

In my case, my experience was so powerful that there was never any difficulty in deciding. The real struggle was in deciding what to make of all the messages I had been receiving from the white community for so long. The question was not whether they were correct or not: the question was: *Why was I receiving them in the first place?*

More questions followed: Why did the dominant white community choose to judge Indians in such a negative — and unjust — way? Why was the white community not open and receptive to the unique and enriching aspects of the native community? How did the white community somehow benefit from the perpetuation of such views? Were there some people who benefited from it more than others? When did this pattern get started? How did the treaties contribute to native peoples being at the bottom of the socio-economic ladder today? How is the white community, through its government, dealing with native peoples today? Is it dealing with them any differently than before?

My questioning was directed initially at understanding historical events, such as treaties that institutionalized relations between natives and non-natives in my area. But when Quebec premier Robert Bourassa announced his grandiose plans for the James Bay hydro-electric project in the early seventies without any attempt to consult with the Cree and Inuit, I began to see that the patterns of a hundred years ago — which had left native peoples marginalized today — were still being employed by our leaders.

And it was at that point that I knew I had to turn my reflection into action.

In the twenty years since, I have devoted myself to the task of understanding my own society and the reasons for its negative treatment of aboriginal peoples. I have focused particularly on land claims in the North because it is here that the relations between natives and non-natives are still in the process of being defined and institutionalized, much as they were during the treaty-making period in the last century.

Only this time, we have a chance to do it differently.

AFTERWORD:
THE PATH AHEAD

ABORIGINAL AND NON-ABORIGINAL relations in Canada are suspended between times. Relations based on racist and colonialist attitudes seem to be dying, and in their place, new relations based on mutual respect and the right to self-determination are being born. Unless there is a major derailing of the constitution process, for example, the Canadian Constitution will soon recognize and enforce aboriginal peoples' inherent right to self-government.

This trend is cause for much celebration and hope, but it is important to remember that the new reality is merely emerging. Indeed, we can expect the burden of our colonialist past to weigh heavily upon us for some time to come. Constitutional revisions recognizing the right of aboriginal peoples to self-government, for example, do no more than set the tone for the establishment of a new relationship. We have taken only our first tentative and wobbly steps towards justice.

The dominant theme of this book has been *journeying* — specifically, the challenge to journey from relationships of discord and mistrust towards relationships of reconciliation and respect. Every article in this book grapples with the question of what it will take to attain relationships which lead to healing and new life for aboriginal peoples and renewal between aboriginal and non-aboriginal peoples. No doubt, this task will be difficult, but there is good reason for hope, for it is aboriginal peoples themselves who have invited the rest of Canada to begin a new journey with them. This book has demonstrated that despite pain and despite living with the day-to-day reality of shattered lives, aboriginal peoples are offering non-aboriginal Canadians — their oppressors — an invitation to start anew.

So how are Canadians to seize this opportunity? And how are they to do so without reverting back to the oppressive and paternalistic patterns of old? Simply by learning to listen to aboriginal people tell us how they have been wronged and to hear them describe the vision they hold for their future and our future together. And further, non-aboriginal Canadians can join ranks with aboriginal peoples to cultivate a new vision to guide us in the forging of a more inclusive society. The stories in this collection have offered us numerous signposts indicating the pathway we must follow. Among them:

We must begin to recognize the authenticity of the pain and disappointment aboriginal people experience. Only when we begin to comprehend and fully acknowledge the magnitude of aboriginal peoples' alienation from themselves, their communities, from their Creator and non-aboriginal society will we have a context for beginning our relationship anew.

We must begin to accept the integrity of an aboriginal vision for life. Aboriginal peoples are trying to find a way to express a distinct and modern identity in a society that allows little room for such distinctiveness. As the Assembly of First Nations has put it,

> The essential point is that each community must have the freedom, power, and resources to draw on its own strengths and tradition, in order to heal the wounds that the past has left and to get on with the great task of rebuilding[1]. . . . [This requires] laws, institutions, mechanisms for governing day-to-day life based on aboriginal culture, values and traditions.[2]

We must seek to ask questions with respect and thereby gain understanding of one another. It is imperative that the hard work of creating a new reality where aboriginal and non-aboriginal peoples relate to one another respectfully and with sensitivity to our mutual responsibility for one another, begin now. Renewal and restoration of this kind begins by establishing linkages of trust and understanding.

We must become open to the reality that aboriginal peoples may have much to teach us, including how to keep the land in good health. Aboriginal peoples assert a responsibility to be stewards or caretakers of the land, which derives from the time of creation. This deep sense of responsibility and attachment to the land, something not easily understood by non-aboriginal peoples, is the source of the considerable urgency aboriginal peoples place upon their participation in redefining a more responsible, environmentally sustainable Canada.

We must look inward and collectively find alternatives to the excesses in our lifestyles that we enjoy as a direct result of having deprived aboriginal peoples of the resources they need. Indeed, Canadians who sense the moral bankruptcy and spiritual vacuousness of materialism may actually find much in the aboriginal vision of life that resonates deeply with our own most dearly held convictions.

Listening leads to empathy and understanding to support. These are important preconditions to a renewed relationship of trust and mutual respect. But listening and understanding must also lead to action. Non-aboriginal Canadians must seize the challenge that aboriginal peoples offer by moving from positions of *support* to active *solidarity*. Solidarity means "standing with" aboriginal peoples, striving together to break divisive perceptions of suspicion, racism and intolerance. And solidarity is about working together tirelessly to transform structures that oppress, push down, and destroy. Indeed, solidarity is about coming to see that the aboriginal and non-aboriginal quests for a better Canada are inextricably bound together. For justice denied to the First Nations translates into a lesser Canada and thus justice denied to all.

To begin our journey of solidarity, then, we must accept the challenge to change our culture of oppression. Though a daunting task, we must not underestimate what we are capable of achieving. One place to start is within our own circles, challenging the popular belief that assimilation is still the answer. And we can do this by telling others why we believe aboriginal peoples have suffered great injustices and why change leading to healing and reconciliation is so desperately needed.

We can also seek to change structures that have historically oppressed and sought to assimilate aboriginal peoples. This would include telling people why we are convinced that Canada would be a better and more just country if we entered into a partnership where aboriginal peoples could freely exercise their inherent and distinct rights. We could suggest, for example, as native groups have suggested for years, that the colonialist Department of Indian Affairs and Northern Development and the assimilationist Indian Act be swept away. And we could encourage all Canadians to commit themselves to a process of fair negotiations leading to meaningful self-government for all Canada's aboriginal peoples.

It is obvious that the clock can't be turned back, but we must not dwell on apologies. What is done, though brutal and tragic, is done. What we must do now — indeed, what this book has challenged us to do now — is stop the suffocation. Two hundred years of insisting that aboriginal peoples adopt a foreign way of life must end now. Today. We must admit we were wrong and then go on together.

In the words of Nishga Rod Robinson,

Today the Aboriginal people and other Canadians stand on opposite shores of a wide river of mistrust and misunderstanding. Each continues to search through the mist for a clear reflection in the waters along the opposite shore. If we are truly to resolve the issues that separate us, that tear at the heart of this great country . . . then we must each retrace our steps through our history to the source of our misperception and misconception of each other's truth. The challenge is to define, clearly, new visions and pragmatic mechanisms that will allow our cultural realities to survive and co-exist. We must seek out those narrow spots near the river's source where our hands may be joined as equal and honourable partners in a new beginning.[3]

TIM SCHOULS

NOTES

JOHN BIRD
Introduction
1. It is difficult to find a term to refer to the original inhabitants of this land as if they were one homogenous group. We have used the terms "native," "aboriginal," "indigenous" and "First Nations" but have avoided "Indian" because of its colonist origin and overtones. Occasionally native authors have chosen to use the term for themselves, or it has been necessary in a historical context. We have referred to specific nations by the names most commonly used at present. We apologize for inevitable inconsistencies that reflect the transitional nature of the times.

ROGER TOWNSHEND
Specific Claims Policy: Too Little Too Late
1. A *limitations of actions* defence relies on laws that provide time-limits (e.g., six years) for initiating legal action.
2. The doctrine of *Crown immunity* means that courts cannot order the Crown to take particular actions. It has been overridden by specific legislation in many cases, but the effects of such legislation do not extend far enough into the past to be useful for many claims of First Nations.
3. See also "Resorting to Court" by Patrick Macklem and Roger Townshend, in this volume.

MURRAY ANGUS
Comprehensive Claims: One Step Forward, Two Steps Back
1. The Dene had signed Treaty No. 8 in 1899 and Treaty No. 11 in 1921, but contested them with some success in the courts in the early 1970s.

PATRICK MACKLEM and ROGER TOWNSHEND
Resorting to Court
1. For a more extended analysis of these issues, see Patrick Macklem, "First Nations Self-Government and the Borders of the Canadian Legal Imagination" (1991), 36 McGill L.J. 382.
2. *St. Catharines Milling and Lumber Co. v. R.*, (1888), 14 App. Cas. 46 (P.C.).

3. The Privy Council (of Britain) was at the time the highest court for Canada. The case was appealed from the Supreme Court of Canada to the Privy Council.
4. *Johnson* v. *McIntosh*, 21 U.S. (8 Wheat.) 543 (1823). Note that other decisions of the U.S. Supreme Court of the same era came to considerably more advantageous conclusions for aboriginal peoples on the same points of law. See *Worcester* v. *Georgia*, 31 U.S. (6 Pet.) 515 (1832).
5. *Bear Island Foundation* v. *Attorney-General of Ontario* (1989), 58 D.L.R. (4th) 117 (Ont.C.A.) aff'd without comment on this point August 15, 1991 (S.C.C.).
6. *Delgamuukw* v. *British Columbia* (1991), 79 D.L.R. (4th) 185 (B.C.S.C.).
7. *Guerin* v. *R.*, [1984] 2 S.C.R. 335, 13 D.L.R. (4th) 390 (S.C.C.).
8. *Attorney General of Canada* v. *Attorney General of Ontario*, [1897] App. Cas. 199 (P.C.).
9. *R.* v. *Sikyea* (1964), 43 D.L.R. (2d) 150 (N.W.T.C.A.), aff'd [1964] S.C.R. 642
10. Department of Indian Affairs and Northern Development, *Statement of the Government of Canada on Indian Policy, 1969* (Ottawa: Queen's Printer, 1969).
11. *Calder* v. *Attorney General of British Columbia*, [1973] S.C.R. 313, 34 D.L.R. (3d) 145.
12. *Re Paulette and Registrar of Titles* (No. 2) (1973), 42 D.L.R. (3d) 8 (N.W.T.S.C.), rev'd on other grounds (1976), 63 D.L.R. (3d) 1 (N.W.T.C.A.); [1977] S.C.R. 628.
13. *Le Chef Max "One-Onti" Gros Louis* v. *La Société de développement de la Baie James*, [1974] R.P. 38, 8 C.N.L.C. 188 (Que. S.C.), rev'd sub nom *La Société de Développement de la Baie James* v. *Chef Robert Kanatewat*, [1975] C.A. 166, 8 C.N.L.C. 373.
14. *Guerin* v. *R.*, [1984] S.C.R. 335, 13 D.L.R. (4th) 321.
15. *Nowegijick* v. *R.*, [1983] 1 S.C.R. 29, 144 D.L.R. (3d) 193, *Simon* v. *R.*, [1985] 2 S.C.R. 387, 24 D.L.R. (4th) 390, *R.* v. *Sioui*, [1990] 1 S.C.R. 1025, 70 D.L.R. (4th) 427.
16. *R.* v. *Sikyea*, supra, note 9.
17. *R.* v. *Sparrow*, [1990] 1 S.C.R. 1075, 70 D.L.R. (4th) 385. For more extended analysis, see Michael Asch and Patrick Macklem, "Aboriginal Rights and Canadian Sovereignty: An Essay on *R.* v. *Sparrow*" (1991), 29 Alberta L. Rev. 498.

LEN SAWATSKY
Self-Determination and the Criminal Justice System
1. See Thomas S. Kuhn, *The Structure of Scientific Revolutions*, 2nd ed. (Chicago: University of Chicago Press, 1970).

2. The following three paragraphs are excerpted from "Developmental Planning Project Report: The Native Harmony and Restoration Centre," prepared by the author's research firm and sponsored by the Interlake Reserves Tribal Council in Manitoba.
3. The articulation of the aboriginal justice paradigm is the author's and has been informed and guided by the assistance of elders and leaders of First Nations in Manitoba and B.C.
4. "Developmental Planning Project Report"
5. Ibid.
6. Taken from statistics provided by the Department of Justice, Corrections Branch, Province of Manitoba
7. Area Crime Statistics, 1986-1988, available from the Planning Branch of the RCMP, D-Division, Winnipeg, Manitoba.
8. Augustine Branigan, *Crimes, Courts and Corrections: An Introduction to Crime and Social Control in Canada* (Toronto: Holt, Rinehart and Winston of Canada, 1984), p. 104.
9. "Correctional Issues Affecting Native Peoples," *Correctional Law Review,* Working Paper no. 7 (Ottawa: Solicitor-General Canada, Ministry Secretariat, February 1988) p. 4.
10. L.F. Meier, *Grants and Denials of Release by Race, by Type, by Release and by Program for the Prairie Region, from January 1, 1979 to December 31, 1985 for all Federal Offenders* (Ottawa: National Parole Board, May 1986).
11. "Developmental Planning Project Report"

MAGGIE HODGSON
Rebuilding Community
1. Derek Clarke, a former dormitory supervisor at the school, was convicted in 1988.

WALDEMAR BRAUL
Ingenika Point: No More Riverboats
1. The research of this article relies on interviews conducted by the author with band members and a transcript of interviews of band members conducted in 1984 by the band. Unreferenced quotations are derived from this research.
2. Robin Fisher, *Contact and Conflict.* (Vancouver: University of British Columbia Press, 1987), pp. 47 and 48.
3. Barbara Green, "After the Flood," *Catalyst,* September, 1988, p. 2.

NIN.DA.WAAB.JIG, WALPOLE ISLAND HERITAGE CENTRE
Walpole Island in 2005: A View from the Future
1. Walpole Island's "Principles for Sustainable Development" are included on p. 184 of this volume.

2. The International Joint Commission is a joint Canada-U.S. quasi-judicial and advisory tribunal on boundary and trans-boundary water issues.
3. BPAC is a bi-national (Canada and U.S.) group of citizens organized in 1988 to develop a comprehensive plan to restore water quality in the St. Clair River.
4. Up until l985, the Indian Act contained a clause [Section 12{1}b] which stated that any legally Indian female who married a non-Indian male lost Indian status for herself and her children.

TIM SCHOULS
Afterword: The Path Ahead
1. p. 19
2. Assembly of First Nations, Commissioners' Report; *First Nations Circle on the Constitution: To the Source*, (Ottawa, Assembly of First Nations, April 1992), p. 17
3. Rod Robinson, Aboriginal title, land rights and the Canadian Constitution, address presented to a University of Victoria symposium, December 1983.

CONTRIBUTORS

MURRAY ANGUS is an Ottawa researcher, writer, analyst and educator who specializes in aboriginal policy. He is the author of *And the Last Shall Be First: Native Policy in an Era of Cutbacks* (Toronto: NC Press 1991), as well as of numerous articles. He has worked extensively for aboriginal organizations.

MICHAEL ASCH is professor of anthropology at the University of Alberta, and teaches anthropology, law and native studies. He has worked extensively with the Dene in the Northwest Territories and has published widely on constitutional issues as they relate to aboriginal rights.

NAPES ASHINI lives in Sheshatshit, Nitassinan. He has spent much of his life hunting and trapping with his family. He and his family and nine other hunters occupied the Minai-nipi bombing range in October of 1990. Napes keeps journals of his time in the country, and writes frequently about Innu life and resistance.

JOANNE BARNABY is executive director of the Dene Cultural Institute. In 1986, she helped to form the Comprehensive Claims Coalition, a lobby group representing nine Indian, Inuit and Métis organizations. She served as national coordinator of the group, which successfully pressured the federal government to change its land claims policy.

JOHN BIRD, a journalist based in southern Ontario, edited *Anglican Magazine* from 1987 to 1992 and *Catalyst*, the national publication of Citizens for Public Justice, from 1982 to 1984. He is currently on the staff of the Anglican Church of Canada to help both native and non-native people deal with the legacy of church-run residential schools for aboriginal people.

WALDEMAR BRAUL is a lawyer in Victoria, British Columbia, where his practice consists of environmental, native and refugee law. In conjunction with Citizens for Public Justice, from 1988 to 1990 he represented the Ingenika Band on reserve land and forestry issues. He has served as director of the B.C. affiliate of Citizens for Public Justice.

LOIS CAPE grew up in Oka, raised her children in Oka, and still lives in Oka. She works with a member of the Micmac nation to provide information and articles on aboriginal issues to a variety of native and alternative media. She also works as a DJ for CKHQ community radio in Kanesatake.

DIANE ENGELSTAD is a freelance writer and editor living in Toronto. She has produced numerous educational resources relating to native concerns, including a cross-cultural study program for church groups on native spirituality. She served as co-director of development for Citizens for Public Justice from 1980 to 1983.

GEORGES ERASMUS is co-chair of the Royal Commission on Aboriginal Peoples. He served as president of the Dene Nation from 1976 to 1983, and as National Chief of the Assembly of First Nations (AFN) from 1985 to 1991.

ELSIE FIDDLER was a member of the Swampy Cree people of northern Manitoba. She was born in Cedar Lake, which was flooded in the early sixties by Manitoba Hydro's Grand Rapids hydro-electric development. She spent most of her adult years in The Pas. Elsie died on November 14, 1990 from complications related to diabetes. She was 40 years old.

ETHEL FUHR is a resident of Wiarton, Ontario, near the Saugeen and Chippewas of the Nawash Reserves. She has been associated with the ecumenical Aboriginal Rights Coalition (Project North) for many years. She is a founding member of Project North Circle, a group of native and non-native people who promote aboriginal justice locally, through education, peaceful protest and civil disobedience.

RENÉ FUMOLEAU, O.M.I., is a priest of the Missionary Oblates of Mary Immaculate. He writes, speaks and conducts seminars and workshops on cross-cultural education. His photographs of life in the North have been exhibited and published widely.

ELLEN GABRIEL, an artist, is a citizen of the Mohawk Nation and the Iroquois Confederacy, born into the Turtle Clan. She was chosen by the women of the Longhouse to serve as a spokesperson for the community of Kanesatake during the Oka crisis, a position she continues to hold. In the language of her Kanienkehaka people her name is Katsi'tsakwas.

BERNICE HAMMERSMITH is a Cree Métis from Beaver River in Ile à la Crosse, Saskatchewan, now living in Saskatoon. She is the provincial secretary of the Métis Society of Saskatchewan (one of three province-wide elected positions) and deals with matters relating to elders, education, women, communications and economic development. She is a management consultant and a member of Native Women of Canada (NWC) through her local organization in Prince Albert.

MAGGIE HODGSON is the executive director of the Nechi Institute. She is a Carrier Indian from B.C., and co-authored *Spirit Weeps* (Edmonton: Nechi Institute, 1988), a book on native-child sexual abuse. She has spoken nationally and internationally on native substance abuse and violence.

BURTON JACOBS is a member of the Chippewa nation of Walpole Island, where he served as chief for five consecutive terms from 1960 to 1970. Walpole Island, on the delta of the St. Clair River in southwestern Ontario, is also home to Potawatomi and Ottawa peoples.

DEAN JACOBS is the executive director of Nin.da.waab.jig, which pro-vides research services to the Walpole Island First Nation. Mr. Jacobs is also a member of the Ontario Ministry of the Environment's Round Table on Environment and Economy.

LORRAINE LAND works for Citizens for Public Justice in Toronto. She is co-chair of the national Aboriginal Rights Coalition and former chair of the Edmonton Ecumenical Coalition for Aboriginal Justice.

PATRICK MACKLEM is an assistant professor of law at the University of Toronto and was formerly a law clerk to Chief Justice Brian Dickson. He teaches and writes on matters relating to constitutional law and First Nations and the law.

STAN MCKAY is a member of the Cree nation from the Fisher Reserve, Manitoba. He is also director of the Dr. Jessie Saulteaux Resource Centre, an ecumenical theological school supported largely by the United Church for aboriginal people interested in professional Chris-tian ministry, in Beausejour, Manitoba. In August 1992 he became the first aboriginal moderator of the United Church of Canada.

JOHN A. OLTHUIS is a partner in a Toronto legal firm. Co-founder of Citizens for Public Justice, he served as research director from 1972 to 1989. In this capacity, he acted as legal counsel to various First Nations and citizens coalitions. He now continues his legal work for First

Nations on comprehensive land claims, specific claims and aboriginal rights and the Canadian Constitution.

PETER PENASHUE lives in Sheshatshit, Nitassinan, where he is currently serving as president of the Innu Nation. He continues to travel extensively with his mother, Elizabeth, acting as her interpreter and joining her in speaking about the Innu struggle.

GARY POTTS is Chief of Teme-Augama Anishnabai First Nation. In 1988 and 1989 the Teme-Augama Anishnabai people blockaded logging roads through their lands in Temagami, Northern Ontario, to prevent loggers from clear-cutting one of the last remaining old-growth forests on the continent.

JOE SANDERS is a legal and political consultant and was advisor to the National Indian Brotherhood (NIB)/AFN from 1981 to 1991.

LEN SAWATSKY runs his own firm specializing in participative research, social analysis, program design and development, training and evaluation. He was assisted in writing his essay by his colleague, Twilla MacDonald.

TIM SCHOULS is currently pursuing a PhD in political science. He was national researcher for Citizens for Public Justice from 1990 to 1992.

LORAN THOMPSON is a member of the Bear Clan and a faithkeeper, a traditional spiritual leader, in the Kanienkehaka or Mohawk First Nation of the community of Akwesasne on the St. Lawrence River. He was charged with assaulting a police officer as a result of the events at Oka and was acquitted in July 1992.

ROGER TOWNSHEND served as chair of the board of directors of Citizens for Public Justice from 1989 to 1992. He plans to begin practising law with John Olthuis in Toronto in 1993, concentrating on aboriginal legal matters. Previously he was senior researcher at the Treaty and Aboriginal Rights Research Centre (Manitoba).